JONATHAN
EDWARDS

SPIRITUAL LEADERS AND THINKERS

JOHN CALVIN

DALAI LAMA (TENZIN GYATSO)

MARY BAKER EDDY

JONATHAN EDWARDS

DESIDERIUS ERASMUS

MOHANDAS GANDHI

AYATOLLAH RUHOLLAH KHOMEINI

MARTIN LUTHER

AIMEE SEMPLE McPHERSON

THOMAS MERTON

SRI SATYA SAI BABA

ELISABETH SCHÜSSLER FIORENZA

EMANUEL SWEDENBORG

SPIRITUAL
LEADERS AND
THINKERS

JONATHAN
EDWARDS

Samuel Willard Crompton

Introductory Essay by
Martin E. Marty, Professor Emeritus
University of Chicago Divinity School

CHELSEA HOUSE
P U B L I S H E R S
A Haights Cross Communications Company

Philadelphia

COVER: Engraving adapted from an oil portrait of Jonathan Edwards, c. 1750–1755, by Joseph Badger.

CHELSEA HOUSE PUBLISHERS

VP, NEW PRODUCT DEVELOPMENT Sally Cheney
DIRECTOR OF PRODUCTION Kim Shinners
CREATIVE MANAGER Takeshi Takahashi
MANUFACTURING MANAGER Diann Grasse

Staff for JONATHAN EDWARDS

EXECUTIVE EDITOR Lee Marcott
EDITOR Kate Sullivan
PRODUCTION EDITOR Noelle Nardone
PHOTO EDITOR Sarah Bloom
SERIES AND COVER DESIGNER Keith Trego
LAYOUT 21st Century Publishing and Communications, Inc.

A Haights Cross Communications ◀▸ Company

www.chelseahouse.com

First Printing

9 8 7 6 5 4 3 2 1

Library of Congress Cataloging-in-Publication Data

Crompton, Samuel Willard.
  Jonathan Edwards / Samuel Willard Crompton.
    p. cm.—(Spiritual leaders and thinkers)
Includes bibliographical references and index.
  ISBN 0-7910-8103-6
  1. Edwards, Jonathan, 1703-1758. I. Title. II. Series.
BX7260.E3C68 2004
285.8'092—dc22

                                        2004010161

All links and web addresses were checked and verified to be correct at the time of publication. Because of the dynamic nature of the web, some addresses and links may have changed since publication and may no longer be valid.

CONTENTS

Foreword

Why become acquainted with notable people when making efforts to understand the religions of the world?

Most of the faith communities number hundreds of millions of people. What can attention paid to one tell about more, if not most, to say nothing of *all*, their adherents? Here is why:

The people in this series are exemplars. If you permit me to take a little detour through medieval dictionaries, their role will become clear.

In medieval lexicons, the word *exemplum* regularly showed up with a peculiar definition. No one needs to know Latin to see that it relates to "example" and "exemplary." But back then, *exemplum* could mean something very special.

That "ex-" at the beginning of such words signals "taking out" or "cutting out" something or other. Think of to "excise" something, which is to snip it out. So, in the more interesting dictionaries, an *exemplum* was referred to as "a clearing in the woods," something cut out of the forests.

These religious figures are *exempla*, figurative clearings in the woods of life. These clearings and these people perform three functions:

First, they define. You can be lost in the darkness, walking under the leafy canopy, above the undergrowth, plotless in the pathless forest. Then you come to a clearing. It defines with a sharp line: there, the woods end; here, the open space begins.

Great religious figures are often stumblers in the dark woods.

We see them emerging in the bright light of the clearing, blinking, admitting that they had often been lost in the mysteries of existence, tangled up with the questions that plague us all, wandering without definition. Then they discover the clearing, and, having done so, they point our way to it. We then learn more of who we are and where we are. Then we can set our own direction.

Second, the *exemplum*, the clearing in the woods of life, makes possible a brighter vision. Great religious pioneers in every case experience illumination and then they reflect their light into the hearts and minds of others. In Buddhism, a key word is *enlightenment.* In the Bible, "the people who walked in darkness have seen a great light." They see it because their prophets or savior brought them to the sun in the clearing.

Finally, when you picture a clearing in the woods, an *exemplum*, you are likely to see it as a place of cultivation. Whether in the Black Forest of Germany, on the American frontier, or in the rain forests of Brazil, the clearing is the place where, with light and civilization, residents can cultivate, can produce culture. As an American moviegoer, my mind's eye remembers cinematic scenes of frontier days and places that pioneers hacked out of the woods. There, they removed stones, planted, built a cabin, made love and produced families, smoked their meat, hung out laundered clothes, and read books. All that can happen in clearings.

In the case of these religious figures, planting and cultivating and harvesting are tasks in which they set an example and then inspire or ask us to follow. Most of us would not have the faintest idea how to find or be found by God, to nurture the Holy Spirit, to create a philosophy of life without guidance. It is not likely that most of us would be satisfied with our search if we only consulted books of dogma or philosophy, though such may come to have their place in the clearing.

Philosopher Søren Kierkegaard properly pointed out that you cannot learn to swim by being suspended from the ceiling on a belt and reading a "How To" book on swimming. You learn because a parent or an instructor plunges you into water, supports you when necessary, teaches you breathing and motion, and then releases you to swim on your own.

Kierkegaard was not criticizing the use of books. I certainly have nothing against books. If I did, I would not be commending this series to you, as I am doing here. For guidance and courage in the spiritual quest, or—and this is by no means unimportant!—in intellectual pursuits, involving efforts to understand the paths others have taken, there seems to be no better way than to follow a fellow mortal, but a man or woman of genius, depth, and daring. We "see" them through books like these.

Exemplars come in very different styles and forms. They bring differing kinds of illumination, and then suggest or describe diverse patterns of action to those who join them. In the case of the present series, it is possible for someone to repudiate or disagree with *all* the religious leaders in this series. It is possible also to be nonreligious and antireligious and therefore to disregard the truth claims of all of them. It is more difficult, however, to ignore them. Atheists, agnostics, adherents, believers, and fanatics alike live in cultures that are different for the presence of these people. "Leaders and thinkers" they may be, but most of us do best to appraise their thought in the context of the lives they lead or have led.

If it is possible to reject them all, it is impossible to affirm everything that all of them were about. They disagree with each other, often in basic ways. Sometimes they develop their positions and ways of thinking by separating themselves from all the others. If they met each other, they would likely judge each other cruelly. Yet the lives of each and all of them make a contribution to the intellectual and spiritual quests of those who go in ways other than theirs. There are tens of thousands of religions in the world, and millions of faith communities. Every one of them has been shaped by founders and interpreters, agents of change and prophets of doom or promise. It may seem arbitrary to walk down a bookshelf and let a finger fall on one or another, almost accidentally. This series may certainly look arbitrary in this way. Why precisely the choice of these exemplars?

In some cases, it is clear that the publishers have chosen someone who has a constituency. Many of the world's 54 million Lutherans may be curious about where they got their name, who the man Martin Luther was. Others are members of a community but choose isolation: The hermit monk Thomas Merton is typical. Still others are exiled and achieve their work far from the clearing in which they grew up; here the Dalai Lama is representative. Quite a number of the selected leaders had been made unwelcome, or felt unwelcome in the clearings, in their own childhoods and youth. This reality has almost always been the case with women like Mary Baker Eddy or Aimee Semple McPherson. Some are extremely controversial: Ayatollah Ruhollah Khomeini stands out. Yet to read of this life and thought as one can in this series will be illuminating in much of the world of conflict today.

Reading of religious leaders can be a defensive act: Study the lives of certain ones among them and you can ward off spiritual—and sometimes even militant—assaults by people who follow them. Reading and learning can be a personally positive act: Most of these figures led lives that we can indeed call exemplary. Such lives can throw light on communities of people who are in no way tempted to follow them. I am not likely to be drawn to the hermit life, will not give up my allegiance to medical doctors, or be successfully nonviolent. Yet Thomas Merton reaches me and many non-Catholics in our communities; Mary Baker Eddy reminds others that there are more ways than one to approach healing; Mohandas Gandhi stings the conscience of people in cultures like ours where resorting to violence is too frequent, too easy.

Finally, reading these lives tells something about how history is made by imperfect beings. None of these subjects is a god, though some of them claimed that they had special access to the divine, or that they were like windows that provided for illumination to that which is eternal. Most of their stories began with inauspicious childhoods. Sometimes they were victimized, by parents or by leaders of religions from which they later broke.

Some of them were unpleasant and abrasive. They could be ungracious toward those who were near them and impatient with laggards. If their lives were symbolic clearings, places for light, many of them also knew clouds and shadows and the fall of night. How they met the challenges of life and led others to face them is central to the plot of all of them.

I have often used a rather unexciting concept to describe what I look for in books: *interestingness.* The authors of these books, one might say, had it easy, because the characters they treat are themselves so interesting. But the authors also had to be interesting and responsible. If, as they wrote, they would have dulled the personalities of their bright characters, that would have been a flaw as marring as if they had treated their subjects without combining fairness and criticism, affection and distance. To my eye, and I hope in yours, they take us to spiritual and intellectual clearings that are so needed in our dark times.

Martin E. Marty
The University of Chicago

1

A Man of God

O that I might be kept from secret faults!

—Diary entry of Jonathan Edwards, 1723

Jonathan Edwards was at home in East Windsor during the summer of 1723. Although a few weeks shy of his twentieth birthday, he had been selected to give the graduation oration at Yale College that fall, and he anxiously prepared and honed his speech-making skills. At the same time, he made entries into his diary that suggest he was rapidly working to improve himself in other ways as well:

> *Resolved,* Whenever I hear any thing spoken in commendation of any person, if I think it would be praiseworthy in me, that I will endeavor to imitate it. July 8, 1723.
>
> *Resolved,* To endeavor, to my utmost, so to act, as I can think I should do, if I had already seen the happiness of Heaven and Hell torments. July 8, 1723.
>
> *Resolved,* When I fear misfortunes and adversity, to examine whether I have done my duty, and resolve to do it, and let the event be just as Providence orders it. I will, as far as I can, be concerned about nothing but my duty and my sin. June 9, and July 13, 1723.
>
> *Resolved,* Not only to refrain from an air of disdain, fretfulness, and anger in conversation, but to exhibit an air of love, cheerfulness and benignity. May 27, and July 13, 1723.[1]

This diary was not a diary in the conventional sense. Edwards did not include in it the minutiae of his daily activites, rather he filled its pages with his spiritual developments. Though some entries were written and rewritten at different times, the private diary and its resolutions provide a better understanding of Jonathan Edwards than almost any of his sermons, which were written for the public.

A DEFINING MOMENT

Yale was in a state of considerable upheaval that summer and fall. Just one year earlier, at the commencement of 1722, the school suffered a great shock when Rector Timothy Cutler and a handful of other instructors announced that they had converted from Congregationalism to Anglicanism, the faith of the Church of

England. Cutler had ended his sermon with a distinctly Anglican prayer method: "And let all the people say Amen." [2]

Few announcements could have been more surprising. The people of New England were the fourth- or fifth-generation descendants of those who moved from Old England. They had crossed the Atlantic Ocean to escape the rule of the Anglican Church. Yale College, like Harvard, specialized in training young men for the Congregational ministry. What would happen if some of those young men now followed the terrible example of Rector Cutler?

The recent action of Rector Cutler put more pressure on Jonathan Edwards. Like all young men at Yale College, he was expected to uphold and promote the Puritan ethic, which involved self-sacrifice, self-denial, and the knowledge that because every person born on Earth was fundamentally depraved, only God's mercy could save men and women from their doom.

As commencement day approached, young Jonathan Edwards felt anxious. He was already highly regarded as a scholar and had served eight months as a pastor to a New York congregation, but this speech was to be delivered to the faculty and students of Yale. The oration could make or break his fledgling career in the ministry. On August 7, while still at home in East Windsor, Connecticut, he confided to his diary:

> To esteem it as some advantage, that the duties of religion are difficult, and that many difficulties are sometimes to be gone through, in the way of duty. Religion is the sweeter, and what is gained by labour is abundantly more precious; as a woman loves her child the more for having brought it forth with travail; and even to Christ Jesus himself his mediatorial glory, his victory and triumph, the kingdom which he hath obtained, how much more glorious is it, how much more excellent and precious, for his having wrought it out by such agonies.[3]

On September 20, the bachelor of arts degree was awarded in the morning session. Then came the master of arts degree, which Jonathan had earned through his work over the previous three years. There was one last task to perform: He had to succeed in his oration, which he would give entirely in Latin. His subject was "A Sinner Is Not Justified in the Sight of God Except Through the Righteousness of Christ Obtained by Faith."[4]

Edwards began:

> The task which concerns us today is of the very highest importance, although of the least difficulty, that is, to defend the truth of the Reformed religion to Protestant and of the Christian religion to Christians.[5]

It would seem that Edwards was bringing coals to Newcastle (an old expression which means bringing something to an area or to a people who already have plenty of it) but Edwards continued:

> Nor do we consider it to be a slight glory to guard that which is assuredly central, both always for the first Christians and for those most recent everywhere who profess the purity of Reformed Christianity.[6]

When Edwards referred to "Reformed Christianity," he meant churches that had undergone reformation in the sixteenth and seventeenth centuries. By this, Edwards separated Protestant churches everywhere from Roman Catholic ones. The Roman Catholic Church had not undergone a reformation and was, according to Edwards, lacking in purity and wholeness.

Edwards, like almost all New England Protestants of his day, considered the Roman Catholic Church a terrible institution and its adherents to be Papists—slavish followers of the Pope in Rome. Ever since Martin Luther had published his statements against the practice of selling indulgences in 1517 (to learn more about this topic, enter the keywords "Martin Luther indulgences" into any Internet search engine and browse the listed websites), those who protested against the abuses of the Roman Catholic

Church had been known as reformers or as simply Protestants (those who protest).

Edwards then tried to put the theory and ideas of Martin Luther into current practice:

> Accordingly, when it is asserted that a sinner is justified by this faith alone, we mean, of course, that God receives the sinner into his grace and friendship for his reason alone, that his entire soul receives Christ in such a way that righteousness and eternal life are offered in an absolutely gratuitous fashion and are provided only because of his reception of Christ.[7]

This may seem wordy, but Edwards was echoing the words of Martin Luther: "Man is saved by Faith alone."

The question of salvation or damnation was one of the hallmarks of the Congregational Church in New England, but it also cast a long shadow over the ministers and their congregations. They wondered how one could truly know whether he was saved or damned and how one should try to love in the world.

Edwards concluded with an expression of his faith:

> Therefore, we now fearlessly assert that as the truth of the Reformed religion is certain, as the first foundation of he gospel is certain, as the mutual consistency of God's attributes is certain, as the incapacity of what is false to be strictly and absolutely demonstrated is certain, and as it is certain that both parts of a contradiction cannot be true, so it is certain that a sinner is not justified in the sight of God except through the righteousness of Christ obtained by faith.

The oration was well received. The audience shouted, "It pleases! It pleases!"[8]

ANOTHER TURNING POINT

In November 1723, Edwards was invited to become a minister to the church of Bolton, Connecticut. This appointment was very much to his father's liking: The Reverend Timothy Edwards wished his only son to be a rural pastor like himself.

Very few records exist from the short time that Jonathan Edwards pastored at Bolton. His internal work and dialogue continued, as demonstrated by his diary:

> Friday night, October 12. I see that there are some things quite contrary to the soundness and perfection of Christianity, in which almost all good men do allow themselves, and where innate corruption has an unrestrained secret vent, which they never take notice of, or think to be no hurt, or cloke under the name of virtue; which things exceedingly darken the brightness, and hide the loveliness of Christianity. Who can understand his errors? O that I might be kept from secret faults![9]

SARAH PIERPONT

At about the same time that he accepted the call to the ministry in Bolton, Edwards wrote the first and only major expression of love in his life. He was a deeply affectionate man, like his father, but he had found little on which to focus his adult affections until he met Sarah Pierpont. This was the third major event in Jonathan Edwards's life to take place in the year 1723.

Born in 1711, Sarah Pierpont was the daughter of the Reverend James Pierpont of New Haven. Her father had been one of the leading men in the formation of the Collegiate School of Connecticut, which had expanded into Yale College. Her father was now dead, and she was under the care of her older brothers. Sarah Pierpont was only 13 when Jonathan Edwards wrote about her:

> They say there is a young lady in [New Haven] who is beloved of that Great Being who made and rules the world, and that there are certain sessions in which this Great Being, in some way or other invisible, comes to her and fills her mind with exceeding sweet delight, and that she hardly cares for any thing, except to mediate on him—that she expects after a

while to be received up where he is, to be raised up out of the world and caught up into heaven; being assured that he loves her too well to let her remain at a distance from his always. . . . She has a strange sweetness in her mind, and singular purity in her affections; is most just and conscientious in all her conduct; and you could not persuade her to do any thing wrong or sinful. . . . She loves to be alone, walking in the field and groves, and seems to have some one invisible always conversing with her.[10]

Edwards was about twenty years old when he found the love of his life. Although he knew he wanted to marry Sarah, he still had to win her affection and wait until she reached a marriageable age. (The couple would finally wed in July 1727, when Sarah was 17 years old.)

Edwards found little comfort or sustenance at the parish in Bolton, Connecticut. He left in the spring of 1724 and returned to Yale as one of the three tutors of the college.

2

A Minister
and His Family

*Through the wonderful mercy and goodness of God
there hath in this place been a very remarkable stirring
and pouring out of the spirit of God . . .*

—Jonathan Edwards,
in a letter to his sister Mary

Born in Connecticut in 1669, Timothy Edwards was the son of a prosperous Hartford merchant. The Edwards family had a distinguished lineage going back to England, but the family fortunes in the New World had been quite mixed. Timothy's father, Richard, had been well known and regarded in his community, but Timothy's mother was a social disgrace. She had had romantic affairs with numerous men in the community and had borne a child out of wedlock. Because the laws governing divorce were quite strict, it was not until 1691 that Richard Edwards was able to divorce his wife.

Young Timothy Edwards had attended Harvard College but was expelled in 1688. The reasons for his expulsion are not known, but it might have had to do with the social stigma created by his mother's behavior. Edwards was fortunate to find a tutor and mentor in Springfield, Massachusetts, who guided him through the Harvard curriculum at a distance, and, in 1694, Harvard granted him his bachelor's and master's degrees on the same day.

ESTHER STODDARD

Having shaken off the ill effects of his mother's reputation, Timothy Edwards was determined to become a model of righteous behavior. To succeed in this endeavor, he would need an excellent spouse, and he found one in Esther Stoddard of Northampton, Massachusetts.

Esther was the daughter of the Reverend Solomon Stoddard. A large, imposing man, Stoddard was called "the Pope of the Valley" by his critics, meaning that he believed himself to be greater than he truly was. Stoddard's Northampton parishioners did not agree with these criticisms. They admired and even adored Stoddard, who had been their pastor since 1669.

Esther Stoddard must have been pleased with Timothy Edwards; as the daughter of Solomon Stoddard, she could have had her pick of the community's unmarried ministers. Timothy Edwards and Esther Stoddard married in Northampton, Massachusetts, in 1694, the same year Timothy was awarded his degrees. The young couple moved about 50 miles down the Connecticut River and settled at East Windsor, Connecticut, on the river's eastern side. There, Timothy Edwards became "the Reverend" Edwards and Esther Stoddard became "Goodwife" Edwards.

LIFE IN EAST WINDSOR

The couple started their family at once. Esther, the eldest child, was born in 1695; Elizabeth came in 1697; Anne was born in 1699; Mary arrived in 1701; and Jonathan, the only boy in the family, was born on October 5, 1703. The Edwardses went on to have six more daughters: Eunice, Abigail, Jerusha, Hannah, Lucy, and Martha. The total count of Edwards children was 11, 10 of them daughters.

JONATHAN EDWARDS'S SISTERS

Although large families were common in colonial America, a ratio of 10 daughters to 1 son was quite unusual. The Edwards sisters must have helped shaped Jonathan's life, and they had unusual life stories of their own.

Esther, the eldest, married the Reverend Samuel Hopkins in 1727, when she was 31. Elizabeth, the second eldest, married at 27. Anne, the third, married at the advanced age of 35. Mary, the fourth, never married but lived to the age of 76, a remarkable accomplishment in a time before modern medicine.

That the Edwards sisters generally married late in life suggests they had a hard time finding suitable husbands. They were tall, attractive, and much more educated than most women of their day. As such, they needed to find men who were their intellectual equals, and this did not come easily.

The six sisters younger than Jonathan were Eunice, Abigail, Jerusha, Hannah, Lucy, and Martha. Four of them married, and diphtheria claimed the lives of Jerusha and Lucy before they were able to marry. One of the most interesting stories about the 10 sisters is that of Martha, the youngest. In 1746, the Reverend Moses Tuttle came to ask the Reverend Timothy Edwards for his daughter's hand. The Reverend Edwards hesitated. Tuttle explained that he had learned that Martha had undergone a conversion experience and would therefore make a good wife. Edwards responded: "Oh yes, yes, Martha is a good girl, But Brother Tuttle, the grace of God will dwell where you or I cannot!"*

*Kenneth P. Minkema, "Hannah and Her Sisters: Sisterhood, Courtship, and Marriage in the Edwards Family in the Early Eighteenth Century," *New England Historical and Genealogical Register*, 1992, p. 47.

Jonathan Edwards obviously grew up in a world of women. His father's word was law in the household, but virtually all of the visible work—cooking, cleaning, scrubbing, and so on—was performed by his mother and sisters. Aside from his father, whose ministerial duties kept him away from home many hours a day, the only male presence young Jonathan experienced was that of "Tim," sometimes mentioned in letters, who was almost certainly the African-American slave of the Edwards family.

It may seem shocking that a minister would have a slave in his home. Slavery never took firm root in New England because its soil and the crops that could be grown there were different from what grown in the Southern colonies. The New England colonists generally farmed squash, pumpkins, potatoes, and corn rather than the labor-intensive crops of the South—tobacco, cotton, and indigo. Therefore, the need for slaves was much less, and New England gained a reputation as being an excellent place for poor men and their families. Still, quite a few of the ministers and leading men in New England towns owned a slave or two. One of the greatest of all the Puritan preachers, the Reverend Cotton Mather of Boston, admitted that he first learned about the idea of inoculation against smallpox from his black slave Onesimus. Records from other towns indicate that the enslavement of people of African descent, though not widespread, was nonetheless accepted.

Jonathan Edwards thus grew up in a home abundant in females and in which there was at least one slave. Still, the most important influence on him, even in his earliest years, was that of his father.

The Reverend Timothy Edwards developed a sterling reputation in East Windsor. He was an extremely conscientious man, as demonstrated by letters he wrote to his wife during his trips away from home. He detailed the tasks to be performed and the manner in which they should be done: He had a great eye for detail. At the same time, he was a deeply loving husband and father and a remarkably devoted pastor. Throughout his life,

Jonathan Edwards felt the pressure of his father's example and strove to live up to the excellent model provided for him.

A CONSCIENTIOUS CHILD

Jonathan Edwards was a precocious child. He learned Latin and Greek at his father's side and matured rapidly in intellectual matters. Timothy Edwards operated a small school within the family home where promising boys from the neighborhood received their education.

The earliest of Jonathan Edwards's surviving letters is dated May 1716, when he was not quite 13 years old. He wrote it to his older sister Mary, who was attending a finishing school in Hatfield, Massachusetts (all of the Edwards daughters received some form of higher education, which was quite unusual for the time). The letter read:

> Dear Sister,
>
> Through the wonderful mercy and goodness of God there hath in this place been a very remarkable stirring and pouring out of the spirit of God, and likewise now is. But I think I have reason to think it is in some measure diminished, but I hope not much. About thirteen [people] have been joined to the church in an estate of full communion . . . I think there comes commonly [on] Mondays above thirty persons to speak with Father about the condition of their souls.[11]

Thirty people each Monday! The Reverend Timothy Edwards was busy indeed. The letter continued:

> It is a time of general health here in this place. There has five persons died in this place since you have been gone, viz, Old Goodwife Rockwell, Old Goodwife Grant, and Benjamin Bancroft who was drowned in a boat many rods from shore wherein were four young women and many others of the other sex, which were very remarkably saved, and the two others which died I suppose you have heard of, Margaret Peck

of the New Town who was once Margaret Stiles hath lost
a sucking babe who died very suddenly and was buried in
this place.[12]

Matters of life, health, and death were constantly on the mind
of early New Englanders. Health was a precious thing, to be
guarded at all times. This was evident in Jonathan's letter:

> Abigail, Hannah, and Lucy have had the chicken pox and are
> recovered, but Jerusha has it now but is almost well. I myself
> sometimes am much troubled with the tooth ache, but these
> two or three last days I have not been troubled with it but very
> little so far as I know the whole family is well except Jerusha.
>
> Sister, I am glad to hear of your welfare so often as I do.
> I should be glad to hear from you by a letter, and therein how
> it is with you as to your crookedness. ["Your crookedness"
> probably means that Mary Edwards suffered from a mal-
> formed spine.]
>
> Your Loving Brother Jonathan Edwards
>
> Father and Mother remember their love unto you. Likewise
> do all my sisters and Mercy and Tim. [Like Tim, Mercy may
> have been a slave of the Edward's family.][13]

As this letter shows, young Jonathan Edwards was an affectionate and dutiful member of his family. He had taken to heart
many of the lessons imparted by his religious parents, and he
already showed a keen interest in matters of religion. He would
soon have new opportunities to test and examine his faith when
he entered Yale College in the autumn of 1716.

3

Yale
College

*I am much reformed with respect to visiting
of friends, and intend to do more at it for
the future than in time past.*

—Letter from Jonathan Edwards to his father

The name Yale conjures images of magnificent ivy-covered brick buildings set on lawns of plush green. Today, Yale University is one of the most prestigious universities in the world. This was not the Yale that Jonathan Edwards attended—at the time, Yale was almost as young a school as Edwards was a person.

Until 1692, Harvard College was the only institution of higher learning in the American colonies. The College of William and Mary, founded in 1692, was the second, but William and Mary had an Anglican faculty that sought to educate Anglican ministers for America. This was entirely unacceptable to Puritan parents from New England, so a quest was underway to establish an alternative to Harvard College.

In the fall of 1701, just two years before Jonathan Edwards was born, a charter was granted for the "Collegiate School of Connecticut." This rather awkward name lasted until about 1718, when the school was renamed Yale College in honor of Elihu Yale, whose donation of books and other possessions was sold to provide the first endowment for the college.[14]

Jonathan Edwards began college in the fall of 1716, two years before the school was renamed. Rather than attending the central campus in New Haven, he took classes at the small branch school at Wethersfield, Connecticut. Wethersfield was only about 10 miles down the Connecticut River from East Windsor, but this small geographical change was quite significant in the life of young Edwards. He was the rather pampered and adored only son in his family, and the move to Wethersfield and away from his home may have made him feel a good deal less special than before.

Elisha Williams, the head of the Wethersfield branch school, was Edwards's cousin on his mother's side. The Williams family had intermarried with the Stoddards several times, and the Williams-Stoddard influence could be felt from Deerfield, Massachusetts, in the north down along the Connecticut River to New Haven, Connecticut, in the south.

Little is known about Jonathan Edwards's time at the Wethersfield branch school. He probably was one of the star pupils, however, and when the Connecticut legislature ordered the Wethersfield students to go to the New Haven campus in 1718, Edwards was among those who followed this command. Edwards then truly became a member of the student body at Yale College, which, though small, was growing in prestige.

Edwards graduated in 1720 at the head of his class of 10 students. He stayed at Yale for his master's degree in theology. The requirements for a master's degree were rather loose in those days: Candidates for the degree studied independently until they were prepared to take their examinations. Edwards had a good deal of time to himself and his studies during the next two years. Indeed, he may have developed habits that were too solitary; his father often admonished him in letters to be friendlier with his fellow students. Jonathan reassured his father that he was being social:

> My condition at the college at present is every way comfortable: I live in very good amity and agreement with my chambermate. There has no new quarrels broke out betwixt me and any of the scholars, though they still persist in their former combination. . . . I am much reformed with respect to visiting of friends, and intend to do more at it for the future than in time past. . . . [15]

Whatever the "former combination" was, it must not have been favorable to Edwards. He may have been locked out or ostracized by his fellow scholars.

SPIRITUAL AWAKENING

Edwards was a naturally solitary individual. He loved to read and believed that the fate of his soul depended on learning and growing all the time. While at Yale, Edwards began to have a religious awakening. Three of his sisters had already been accepted as full members of the East Windsor Church based on their testimonies of saving grace, a requirement for membership; now Jonathan began to have his first stirrings. Unfortunately, he did not keep a diary at the time, and the only record of the events comes from a narrative he wrote nearly 20 years later:

> Absolute sovereignty is what I love to ascribe to God. But my first conviction was not so.
>
> The first instance that I remember of that sort of inward, sweet delight in God and divine things that I have lived in much since, was on reading those words, 1 Timothy I:17. Now unto the King eternal immortal, invisible, the only wise God, be honor and glory forever and ever, Amen. As I read the words, there came into my soul, and was as it were diffused through it, a sense of the glory of the Divine Being; a new sense, quite different from any thing I ever experienced before.[16]

The absolute sovereignty of God was one of the principles of the Puritan faith, derived from the writings of the sixteenth-century Frenchman John Calvin. In his *Institutes of the Christian Religion*, published in 1536, Calvin had devoted significant attention to the omnipotent (all-powerful) and omniscient (all-knowing) qualities of God. According to Calvin, because God was absolute sovereign of the universe, no man could ever truly know whether he was saved or damned. God's omniscience, however, meant that God had decided before a person was even born whether that person would be damned or saved (to learn more about this topic, enter the keywords "John Calvin Institutes" into any Internet search engine and browse the listed websites).

Edwards had known about Calvin and the principle of pre-destination since he was a young boy. Now, at about the age of 20, he suddenly had a breakthrough in religious understanding, and he could indeed see God for the omnipotent and omniscient being that God truly was. Edwards wrote of this understanding:

> From about that time, I began to have a new kind of appre-hensions and ideas of Christ, and the work of redemption, and the glorious way of salvation by him. An inward, sweet sense of these things, at times, came into my heart; and my

soul was led away in pleasant views and contemplations of them. And my mind was greatly engaged to spend my time in reading and meditating on Christ, on the beauty and excellency of his person, and the lovely way of salvation by free grace in him. I found no books so delightful to me as those that treated of these subjects. Those words, Cant. ii:1 used to be abundantly with me, I am the Rose of Sharon, and the Lily of the valleys.[17]

So far this was a "traditional" narrative of salvation. Edwards, like many Puritans, struggled with the great paradox of his faith. As spiritual descendants of Martin Luther and John Calvin, Puritans held salvation by God's grace and predestination as their major beliefs. Puritans like Edwards struggled with the belief that an upright and pious life was absolutely necessary for salvation but that such a life did not guarantee salvation.

CITY LIFE

In the autumn of 1722, Jonathan Edwards's religious awakening led him to New York, where he served as pastor of a small Presbyterian church. Edwards boarded in the home of Mr. John Smith and his mother, whom he found to be most pious. The next six or eight months were Edwards's only time spent in a metropolitan environment, yet they seem to have played an important part in his spiritual development. Many years later, he recounted the changes that took place within him as he experienced life in New York City:

> On January 12, 1723, I made a solemn dedication of myself to God, and wrote it down; giving up myself, and all that I had to God; to be for the future in no respect my own; to act as one that had no right to himself, in any respect.[18]

Edwards was a young man, only 19 years old. He had been raised, however, in a deeply religious home, and it was natural that God would be first in his thoughts. Now, in 1723, Edwards made a vow to place God first in all matters:

> And solemnly [I] vowed to take God for my whole portion and felicity; looking on nothing else as any part of my happiness, nor acting as if it were; and his law for the constant rule of my obedience; engaging to fight with all my might, against the world, the flesh and the devil, to the end of my life.[19]

God and the devil both were very real presences for the people of colonial America. The Salem Witch Trials had taken place only 30 years earlier, and many, if not most, Americans believed in the power of the devil as well as that of God.

Even in the city of New York, Edwards found time and space to be in communion with Nature:

> I very frequently used to retire into a solitary place, on the banks of Hudson's river, at some distance from the city, for contemplation on divine things, and secret[ly] converse with God; and had many sweet hours there. Sometimes Mr. Smith and I walked there together, to converse on the things of God; and our conversation used to turn much on the advancement of Christ's kingdom in the world, and the glorious things that God would accomplish for his church in the latter days. I had then, and at other times the greatest delight in the holy scriptures [probably either the Book of Common Prayer or the King James Bible], of any book whatsoever. Oftentimes in reading it, every word seemed to touch my heart.[20]

He may have seen in New York City a life and way of being that was quite different from what he knew. Raised in the country and educated by his father and then by professors at Yale, Edwards had heard the word of God throughout his entire life. Now he was exposed to the sights and sounds of urban life, the bustle of horses and carts, and the hawking of tobacco and sugar.

Just three months after he made his solemn resolutions, Edwards was called away from New York City. It is unclear whether his reverend father required him to go home to Connecticut or whether the small Presbyterian church in Manhattan was unable to support its young minister. In either case, Edwards left:

> I came away from New York in the month of April, 1723, and had a most bitter parting with Madam Smith and her son. My heart seemed to sink within me at leaving the family and the city, where I had enjoyed so many sweet and pleasant days. I went from New York to Wethersfield, by water and as I sailed away, I kept sight of the city as long as I could.[21]

His sojourn in the city over, the country boy returned home.

4

Northampton

We have not been so much corrupted with vice,
as most other parts.

—Edwards to the Reverend Benjamin Colman of Boston

Northampton, Massachusetts, was a place of about 200 families and perhaps a population of 1,000 in 1727. First settled in 1654, Northampton was one mile due west of a bend in the Connecticut River.

Edwards arrived in Northampton early in 1727 and was ordained in February. For the next two years, he alternated in preaching with Solomon Stoddard, his renowned grandfather. It is possible that Edwards learned more in those 24 months than in all his years of formal education combined.

Age had dimmed Stoddard's sight, but his mind was as sharp as ever. He had been something of a religious rebel since his youth. Coming to Northampton in 1669, Stoddard had formulated the novel idea of allowing Half-Way Covenant members (those who were not full members of the church) access to the Lord's Table, or Holy Communion. Stoddard had argued in speech and in print that communion could serve as a device to assist full conversion.

Stoddard and Edwards now worked together. The contrast must have been very noticeable. The former was 85 years old, and the latter was only 23. Quite a few people around town expressed it in biblical terms: Edwards had become the Elisha to his grandfather's Elijah.

About a decade after he arrived in the town, Edwards expressed his early views of Northampton:

> The people of the country in general, I suppose, are as sober, and orderly, and good sort of people, as in any part of New England; and I believe they have been preserved the freest by far, of any part of the country from error and variety of sects and opinions.[22]

Though he did not say so explicitly, Edwards probably meant that the people of Northampton, and of Hampshire County as a whole, were not given to experimenting with new religious groups or sects. Edwards was a strict Calvinist minister, and it distressed him to see other New Englanders breaking away from the faith of their ancestors. He went on:

> Our being so far within the land, at a distance from sea-ports, and in a corner of the country, has doubtless been one reason why we have not been so much corrupted with vice, as most other parts. But without question, the religion and good order of the country, and their purity in doctrine, has, under God, been very much owing to the great abilities, and eminent piety, of my venerable and honored grandfather Stoddard.[23]

Edwards also described his grandfather's ministry:

> He continued in the work of the ministry here from his first coming to town, near sixty years. And as he was eminent and renowned for his gifts and grace, so he was blessed, from the beginning, with extraordinary success in his ministry, in the conversion of many souls. He had five harvests as he called them: The first was about fifty-seven years ago; the second about fifty-three years; the third about forty; the fourth about twenty-four; the fifth and last about eighteen years ago. Some of these times were much more remarkable than others, and the ingathering of souls more plentiful.[24]

The Reverend Stoddard died in 1728, and leadership of the Northampton parish went to Jonathan Edwards. He was very conscious of having to fill the big shoes of his grandfather, and would continually remind his parishioners how fortunate they were to have had Stoddard as their minister.

RELIGIOUS CRISES

The "ingathering of souls," Edwards referred to were his congregants' testimonies of moments of saving grace, a hallmark of the Puritan faith. To gain admittance to full church membership, young Puritans gave witness to moments or episodes in which they felt the power of God and of God's saving grace.

The Puritans were English men and women who generally detested the Anglican Church. They crossed the Atlantic Ocean in the early seventeenth century to escape from that church and to set up a Puritan commonwealth in the New World. They succeeded to such an extent that for the first 80 years of settlement in New England, the Puritan church ran the government as well as spiritual affairs.

The Puritans faced more than one crisis along the way, however. In the early 1660s, it became apparent that far fewer members of the new generation had experienced moments of "saving grace," or personal evidence of salvation. Until then, only persons who could relate such stories were admitted to full church membership. If the policy of only admitting members who had those experiences continued, the church soon would run out of members. Therefore, in 1664, the "Half-Way Covenant" was adopted to allow the sons and daughters of full church members to be granted provisional church memberships without testifying to a moment of saving grace.

A second major crisis arose in 1692, when a group of young girls in Salem, Massachusetts, accused older women of being witches and casting spells meant to bring sickness and harm. Puritan leaders were dismayed by the situation. They believed in the biblical admonition that "Thou shalt not suffer a witch to live." Due to this belief, in addition to increasing accusations and the hysteria they caused, about 20 persons were executed in the fall of 1692. The Puritan church never fully recovered from this event: Many New Englanders began to view the leadership and the church itself with suspicion (to learn more about this episode in history, enter the keywords "Salem witch trials" into any Internet search engine and browse the listed websites).

In his *Narrative of Many Surprising Conversions,* Jonathan Edwards alluded to the difficulties that the Puritan church experienced after about the year 1700. It seemed that the younger members of the church were behaving in a way that Edwards considered immoral:

> After the last of these [ingatherings], came a far more degenerate time, (at least among young people) I suppose, than ever

before. . . . Just after my grandfather's death, it seemed to be a time of extraordinary dullness in religion: Licentiousness for some years greatly prevailed among the youth of the town; they were many of them very much addicted to night walking, and frequenting the tavern, and lewd practices, wherein some by their example exceedingly corrupted others. It was their manner very frequently to get together in conventions of both sexes, for mirth and jollity, which they called frolicks; and they would often spend the greater part of the night in them, without any regard to order in the families they belonged to: And indeed family government did too much fail in the town.[25]

Edwards was disappointed with the level of faith shown by the people of Northampton. Had they not experienced the preaching of Solomon Stoddard for the past 60 years? Why were they not more penitent, more attuned to the word of God?

There are two likely answers. First and foremost, the people of Northampton were "burned out" from years of Solomon Stoddard's intense preaching. Too many harsh Calvinist messages had come from Stoddard's pulpit, and the people wanted relief.

Second, and just as important, Northampton as a town and the Connecticut River Valley as a whole were undergoing an economic crisis. The painstaking research of Patricia J. Tracy has shown that Northampton outgrew its original settlement area by about 1700 and that there were no more lots to be had. A young man in Northampton could not acquire land and a home unless either his father died or he was willing to uproot and move elsewhere. There was a remedy in the future—Northampton would eventually expand and have sister communities called Southampton, Westhampton, and Easthampton—but this did not happen for another 50 years, and at that time, there was little opportunity for the young people of the town.

REVIVAL

Edwards described a change that took place in the winter of 1733–1734:

> There began to appear a remarkable religious concern at a little village belonging to the congregation, called Pascommuck . . . , where a few families were settled, at about three miles distance from the main body of the town. At this place a number of persons seemed to be savingly wrought upon. In the April following, Anno 1734, there happened a very sudden and awful death of a . . . youth; who being violently seized with a pleurisy, and taken immediately very delirious, died in about two days; which . . . much affected many young people. This was followed with another death of a young married woman, who had been considerably exercised in mind, about the salvation of her soul, before she was ill, and was in great distress in the beginning of her illness, but seemed to have satisfying evidences of God's saving mercy to her, before her death; so that she died very full of comfort, in a most earnest and moving manner, warning and counseling others.[26]

Although almost every New Englander at the time had had brothers, sisters, uncles, aunts, or cousins who had died, these two deaths in 1734 invaded the minds of the people of Northampton. As a result, they became more receptive to hearing God's word. Edwards wrote of this time:

> In the fall of the year, I proposed it to the young people, that they should agree among themselves to spend the evenings after lectures, in social religion, and to that end to divide themselves into several companies to meet in various parts of the town; which was accordingly done, and those meetings have been since continued, and the example imitated by elder people.[27]

It seems clear that a genuine revival began and that it started with the efforts of young people rather than the middle-aged or elderly. This alone was a favorable sign, and it indicated a turning point to Edwards and other ministers in the valley. Perhaps the time had come when the Lord would show himself to his people of New England.

JONATHAN EDWARDS, AUTHOR

Jonathan Edwards had few personal weaknesses. Money had no charm for him; neither did the applause of the crowd. He had been taught in a tough school—his father's—and he did not need to win approval from his parishioners. He did have one great ache, though, and that was to be acknowledged as an intellectual both at home in America and abroad in Europe. Since his days at Yale, when he read the writings of philosopher John Locke—one of the fathers of the Enlightenment—Edwards had

THE ENLIGHTENMENT

The intellectual movement known as the Enlightenment is often considered as being the start of modernity.

Toward the end of the seventeenth century, a number of philosophers and scientists laid the foundations for a more rational view of the world as a whole. John Locke wrote about human understanding, Isaac Newton described a new type of physics and calculus, and Baron von Leibniz did something quite similar in Germany. Together, these men and their contemporaries set the stage for a new way of looking at the world and the universe.

All of these men were interested in North America, seeing the relatively recently discovered continent as a great unspoiled land where new theories could be tested because neither the people nor the landscape had yet been influenced by negative patterns of human behavior. One of John Locke's most famous lines, "In the beginning all the world was America," captured the spirit of this view.

The ideas of Newton, Locke, Leibniz, and others spread across America rather slowly but thrived on arrival at Yale College. Edwards therefore was exposed to the ideas of the Enlightenment earlier than many of his contemporaries. Throughout his life, Edwards displayed a level of interest in scientific matters that almost equaled his interest in the spirit. Indeed, for him, these two realms were not separate or at war with one another; they combined to form a picture of God's will for humankind and for the world as a whole.

understood the power of the printed word. He wanted to be another Locke, another person who changed the world with the power of his pen.

In the spring of 1735, Edwards wrote a long letter to the Reverend Benjamin Colman in Boston. Colman had been a contemporary of the Reverend Solomon Stoddard, and Edwards felt confident that Colman would approve of the way the revival had taken hold in the Northampton area. Edwards may have suggested that the letter be published, or Colman may have taken it on himself; either way, the letter was later expanded and published in London and Boston, fulfilling a major ambition of Jonathan Edwards the writer.

In the letter, Edwards described the wonderful workings of God in Northampton:

> People are brought off from inordinate engagedness after the world, & have been ready to run into the other extreme of too much neglecting their worldly business & to mind nothing but religion. Those that are under convictions are put upon it earnestly to enquire what they shall do to be saved, & diligently to use appointed means of Grace, and apply themselves to all known duty.[28]

Edwards almost seems to complain about the involvement in the Spirit rather than the things of the flesh! He went on:

> There is an alteration made in the town in a few months that strangers can scarcely [be] conscious of; our Church I believe was the largest in New England before, but persons lately have thronged in, so that there are very few adult persons left out. There have been a great multitude hopefully converted, too many, I find, for me to declare abroad with credit to my judgment.[29]

When Edwards wrote that his church had been the largest in New England, he meant in terms of members who were admitted to the Lord's Supper (because of the relaxed policy of Solomon Stoddard). This should have been judged a major success, but Edwards already was expressing uneasiness that the new conversions had taken place too rapidly. He feared there had not been time enough for him to properly judge each and every case.

Then, as if to present a counterpoint to this concern, Edwards told a story of conversion:

> There is a pious woman in this town that is a very modest bashful person, that was moved by what she heard of the experiences of others earnestly to seek to God to give her more clear manifestations of himself, and seek evidences of her own good estate, & God answered her request, and gradually gave her more & more of a sense of his glory & love, which she had with intermissions for several days, till one morning the week before last she had it to a more than ordinary degree.[30]

Edwards concluded on a hopeful note:

> Thus sir I have given you a particular account of this affair which Satan has so much misrepresented in the country. This is a true account of the matter as far as I have opportunity to [know], & suppose I am under greater advantages to know than any person living.[31]

Edwards signed the letter on May 30, 1735. Four days later, he wrote a postscript:

> Since I wrote the following letter, there has happened a thing of a very awful nature in the town; My uncle Hawley, the last Sabbath morning, laid violent hands on himself, & put an end to his life, by cutting his own throat. He had been for a considerable time greatly concerned about the condition of his soul; till, by the ordering of a sovereign Providence he was suffered to fall into deep melancholy, a distemper that the family are very prone to.[32]

Joseph Hawley was Edwards's uncle by marriage. He was the most successful merchant in Northampton and had been highly esteemed by his fellow parishioners. No matter what gloss Edwards attempted to put on it, Hawley's suicide was a grave loss to the town and to the revival movement occurring within it.

5

The Great Awakening

Every horse seemed to go with all his might to carry his rider to hear news from heaven for the saving of Souls.

—Farmer Nathan Cole, describing the rush
to attend a sermon by George Whitefield

Northampton had had its own special awakening. Now the movement spread to Boston and to other parts of the colonies.

Edwards was discouraged by 1737. The flame of the awakening of 1734–1735 appeared to have burned out, and the people of Northampton were more concerned with building a new church than with the spiritual feeling they needed to fill it. A remarkable event took place on March 13, 1737, however—an event that appeared to boost both Edwards's spirits and the energy of his congregation:

> We in this town were, the last Lord's day, (March 13th) the spectators, and many of us the subjects, of one of the most amazing instances of Divine preservation, that perhaps was ever known in the world. Our meeting-house is old and decayed, so that we have been for some time building a new one, which is yet unfinished. It has been observed of late, that the house we have hitherto met in, has gradually spread at the bottom; the sills and walls giving way . . . . So that in the midst of the public exercise in the forenoon, soon after the beginning of the sermon, the whole gallery—full of people, with all the seats and timbers, suddenly and without any warning—sunk, and fell down, with the most amazing noise, upon the heads of those that sat under, to the astonishment of the congregation. The house was filled with dolorous shrieking and crying; and nothing else was expected than to find many people dead, or dashed to pieces.[33]

Edwards explained that although many people were injured, none of the injuries were serious, and not a single person had been killed. He went on:

> It seems unreasonable to ascribe it to any thing else but the care of Providence, in disposing the motions of every piece of timber, and the precise place of safety where every one should sit and fall.[34]

While this event should have brought Edwards and his congregants closer, however, Edwards still despaired of them.

They quarreled with each other over petty matters such as who was to be seated where in the church. The final arrangement, of which Edwards disapproved, was that wealth, age, and social usefulness would be the criteria by which people would be placed in their pews.

GEORGE WHITEFIELD

The catalyst for a new awakening was a young British churchman, George Whitefield. Born in Gloucester, England, in 1714, Whitefield was a decade younger than Edwards. Whitefield grew up in a very pious family, but he was not especially religious until the middle of his studies at Cambridge University. Looking back on his days as a student, Whitefield later confessed he had been an impious youth but had been saved by a direct experience of the Holy Spirit, which he described as a physical sensation in his body. From that time forward, Whitefield became one of the great preachers of his day.

Whitefield was a member of and a minister in the Church of England. This was the same church that the Puritans had left England in order to escape and the one that Yale had been so scandalized to lose its rector to in 1722. Whitefield, however, was a new and different type of Anglican who specialized in reaching large crowds. In 1738, he gave a sermon to 4,000 people, the largest outdoor sermon preached up to that time in England. Now, in 1740, he was in America for the second time, and Jonathan Edwards wanted the benefit of his presence.

Whitefield first went to Boston, where he enjoyed one of the greatest triumphs of his long career. He stayed in the city for two weeks, preaching every day, and was constantly waited upon by Governor Jonathan Belcher. Whitefield was at the very peak of his oratorical powers. In the third week of September, he headed to the Edwards home.

The entire Edwards family was there to greet him. Whitefield later reflected on the family:

Felt a wonderful satisfaction in being at the house of Mr. Edwards. He is a Son himself, and hath also a daughter of Abraham for his wife. A sweeter couple I have not yet seen. Their children were dressed not in silks and satins, but plain, as becomes the children of those who, in all things, ought to be examples of Christian simplicity. She is a woman adorned with a meek and quiet spirit, talked feelingly and solidly of the things of God, and seemed to be such a [helpmate] for her husband, that she caused me to renew those prayers, which, for many months, I have put up to God, that he would be pleased to send me a daughter of Abraham to be my wife. I find, upon many accounts, it is my duty to marry. Lord I desire to have no choice of my own. Thou knowest my circumstances; thou knowest I only desire to marry in and for thee.[35]

Whitefield had recently learned that the English woman he loved had rejected his offer of marriage. He was saddened by this response and appears to have seen in Jonathan and Sarah Edwards a model for the type of relationship he desired.

Whitefield left Northampton a month later. He rode slowly south, retracing his steps as far as Springfield. The Reverend Edwards accompanied him, and the two men rode to East Windsor, Connecticut, where they visited Edwards's aged parents. Whitefield was as impressed with this family as he had been at Northampton:

I believe a true disciple and minister of the Lord Jesus Christ. After exercise, we supped at the house of old Mr. Edwards. His wife was as aged, I believe, as himself, and I fancied that I was sitting in the house of a Zacharias and Elisabeth.[36]

Whitefield rode on to Middletown, Connecticut, where he preached on Wednesday, October 23.

To this point, historians have access only to the journals of Whitefield and Edwards. Once the pair arrived in Middletown, Connecticut, however, a farmer named Nathan Cole heard

Whitefield preach and later wrote about the event, providing us with a unique source. Cole recorded:

> Then on a sudden, in the morning about 8 or 9 of the clock there came a messenger and said Mr. Whitefield preached at Hartford and Weathersfield yesterday and is to preach at Middletown this morning at ten of the clock, I was in my field at work, I dropped my tool that I had in my hand and ran home to my wife telling her to make ready quickly to go and hear Mr. Whitefield. . . .
>
> When I saw Mr. Whitefield come upon the scaffold he looked almost angelical; a young, slim, slender youth before some thousands of people with a bold undaunted countenance, and my hearing how God was with him every where he went as he came along it solemnized my mind; and put me into a trembling fear before he began to preach; for he looked as if he was cloathed with authority from the Great God; and a sweet solemn solemnity sat upon his brow. And my hearing him preach, have me a heart wound; By God's blessing: my old foundation was broken up, and I saw that my righteousness would not save me.[37]

Nathan Cole was one of thousands of Anglo Americans caught up in the throes of the First Great Awakening. (Anglo American is the term used to describe settlers who came to the New World from England.) Whitefield's preaching had a powerful effect on them, but it took the combined efforts of Whitefield and Edwards to create the Awakening.

The Great Awakening (now called the First Great Awakening; the second followed in the 1790s) was a widespread religious revival that took place in the American colonies from about the 1720s to the 1740s. Jonathan Edwards and George Whitefield were among the leaders in the final years of the movement. Religious leaders worried that people's attitudes had become too complacent about religion and about human nature, tending to ignore the darker aspects of humanity. A result of the Great Awakening was the separation of Puritans into the "New Light" (evangelical Calvinists) and the "Old Light" (those who retained more moderate beliefs). Jonathan Edwards is considered a New Light (to learn more about this division, enter the keywords " 'great awakening' 'new light' 'old light' " into any Internet search engine and browse the listed websites).

Jonathan Edwards was less certain than George Whitefield about the nature of the Great Awakening. Then again, as in other matters, Edwards had an advantage over Whitefield: He had been involved in the evaluation of religious awakening throughout his entire life.

During the early part of 1741, Edwards rejoiced to learn of George Whitefield's continued success. The British minister finally embarked for home; he would return to North America five more times in his career, for a total of seven transatlantic crossings.

Edwards was now more convinced than ever that the time would soon come when the forces of light would battle those of the Antichrist. Always interested in numbers and prophecy, Edwards had made some predictions of his own. The Antichrist, which he identified as the Papacy in Rome, would fall sometime before the year 2000, after which the era of Christ and the light of God would commence. Although it was a long time until then, Edwards was eager, always urging his fellow Christians to battle the enemy here and now.

The summer of 1741 was, in several ways, the high point of Jonathan Edwards's career. He was an internationally known scholar, thinker, and preacher, and his work in encouraging the Northampton revival of 1734–1735 had helped bring about the Great Awakening, which had just begun. Even as his career grew larger and more respected, however, Edwards felt despondent about his own parish. The people of Northampton had heard him preach on the same topics for so long that they seemed deaf to his entreaties. Consequently, Edwards stepped up his use of rhetoric. He may even have tried in some way to emulate George Whitefield's remarkable use of hyperbole and excitement: 1741 was the year in which he delivered his most poignant and terrifying sermon, the one for which he remains most famous today.

"SINNERS IN THE HANDS OF AN ANGRY GOD"

Early in July 1741, the Reverend Jonathan Edwards set out from Northampton. He headed south on horseback for Enfield, Connecticut.

The weather was fine. New England had recently emerged from the worst part of what has since been called the "Little Ice Age." New England and most of continental America were in a new warming trend, and Edwards probably felt the heat as his horse plodded southward. He was, in a sense, headed home. Edwards may have worked on his sermon, at least in his mind, during that long ride. He was perfecting phrases, smoothing and enlivening his text. Edwards was already known as one of the finest and subtlest of all American theologians, but he was not

GEORGE WHITEFIELD'S LATER CAREER

George Whitefield's visit to the Edwards family in Northampton came during the second of his seven round-trip transatlantic journeys. This was in a time when most people were proud to boast that they had survived one or two such trips.

Sadly, the last five trips did not produce the furor or excitement of the first two. Whitefield's preaching style did not deteriorate and the passion of his message continued as strong as ever, but Americans proved much less receptive to the message after about 1745.

The last of Whitefield's voyages took place in 1770, 12 years after Jonathan Edwards's death. By this time, the Anglo-American friendship and understanding had begun to fray; Whitefield arrived in America just months after the famous Boston Massacre of March 1770.

Whitefield, who had been one of the architects of the Anglo-American relationship, could not believe that it had unraveled. He preached as loudly and energetically as ever, but he interjected political topics as well, urging Americans to remain faithful to King George III.

Whitefield collapsed in Newburyport, Massachusetts. He had suffered from asthma for many years, and doctors had urged him to take on a lighter preaching schedule. Whitefield died and was buried in the coastal New England town. His passing was yet another broken bond between England and her American colonies. There was no successor to his role as the evangelical preacher of the eighteenth century.

known for the power of his voice. Rather, he spoke in calm, even tones, and his audience, knowing him to be a man of great depth, strained to catch every word.

There was already a tradition of eloquence in Colonial America. Early Puritan speakers like Governor John Winthrop and Increase Mather and his son Cotton had set a rather high standard. Cotton Mather, in particular, was known for his ability as a speaker and for his prolific writing: He had authored about 400 books, pamphlets, and issues during his life (1663–1728). Now, in 1741, Edwards was at a moment when he could take his place among the great New England theologians.

Edwards cantered into Enfield, Connecticut, and on July 8, he delivered his sermon entitled "Sinners in the Hands of an Angry God" (see Appendix for full text). Such a bleak title was not unusual for the time. The most famous poem in Colonial New England was Michael Wigglesworth's "Day of Doom," published in 1663 (see Appendix). Other sermon titles and book titles also showed a deep concern with saving grace.

God and the devil were real, living entities for most of the people of New England in 1741. Many British colonists viewed life as a play in which the devil and God wrestled for dominion in the world, each trying to win souls for Hell and Heaven. Only 49 years earlier, the people and judges of Massachusetts had condemned 20 persons to death in Salem on suspicion of witchcraft. There had been no witchcraft episodes since 1692, but the people of New England were ever watchful. They heeded their preachers, who warned them that the devil acted when good people were lulled to sleep or complacency.

Edwards began his sermon by quoting from the Bible, a traditional introduction to a sermon. His quote for "Sinners in the Hands of an Angry God" was excerpted from chapter 32, verse 35 of the Book of Deuteronomy: "Their foot shall slide in due time." Edwards began:

> In this verse is threatened the vengeance of God on the wicked
> unbelieving Israelites, who were God's visible people, and

who lived under the means of grace; but who, notwithstanding all God's wonderful works towards them, remained (as
verse 28) void of counsel, having no understanding in them.
Under all the cultivations of heaven, they brought forth bitter
and poisonous fruit; as in the two verses next preceding the
text. The expression I have chosen for my text, their foot
shall slide in due time, seems to imply the following things,
relating to the punishment and destruction to which these
wicked Israelites were exposed.[38]

Edwards explained that all humans, no matter how correct
or upright they might appear, are liable to slip and fall at any
moment. Even the most righteous can fall at any time because of
their confidence in themselves rather than their faith in God.
After all, the Israelites, whom he mentioned, were the original
"chosen people" of God. If they failed, as the Bible clearly stated,
then what hope was there for the people of New England?

Edwards continued:

The observation from the words that I would now insist
upon is this. "There is nothing that keeps wicked men at any
one moment out of hell, but the mere pleasure of God." By
the mere pleasure of God, I mean his sovereign pleasure, his
arbitrary will, restrained by no obligation, hindered by no
manner of difficulty, any more than if nothing else but
God's mere will had in the least degree, or in any respect
whatsoever, any hand in the preservation of wicked men
one moment.[39]

Edwards's use of the word *sovereign* had special meaning for
his listeners. They were American Protestants, to be sure, but
they traced their spiritual lineage to Martin Luther and John
Calvin, both of whom had emphasized the great sovereign
power of the Lord. If men and women were saved, according to
Luther and Calvin, it was because of God's will for them, not
because of any worthiness on their parts.

Edwards continued:

> So that it is not because God is unmindful of their wicked-
> ness, and does not resent it, that he does not let loose his hand
> and cut them off. God is not altogether such a one as them-
> selves, though they may imagine him to be so. The wrath of
> God burns against them, their damnation does not slumber;
> the pit is prepared, the fire is made ready, the furnace is now
> hot, ready to receive them; the flames do now rage and glow.
> The glittering sword is whet, and held over them, and the pit
> hath opened its mouth under them.[40]

Where did this harsh language come from? Was this the same
Edwards renowned for his goodness toward his family and his
faithful service to his Northampton community?

One of the best clues to this comes from the work of George
Marsden, whose monumental biography of Edwards was published in 2003. Marsden, like many other writers, acknowledged
that Edwards was a man of calmness, dignity, and compassion
but also that Edwards knew plenty of woe in his family growing
up. Timothy Edwards had been an exemplary father and
the immediate family had known peace and prosperity, but
Edwards's grandmother had been a nymphomaniac, his great
uncle had killed one of his great-aunts with an axe, and another
great-aunt had killed one of her children. Thus, Jonathan
Edwards had plenty of material in the back of his mind with
which to create the horrible scenes of "Sinners in the Hands of
an Angry God."

Edwards was far from finished admonishing the congregation:

> God has laid himself under no obligation, by any promise to
> keep any natural man out of hell one moment. God certainly
> has made no promises either of eternal life, or of any deliverance
> or preservation from eternal death, but what are contained in
> the covenant of grace, the promises that are given in Christ.[41]

This was one of the key points of Edwards's religious philosophy. God owes no man anything and makes no promises.

Whatever a person receives comes from God's goodness and grace rather than from any contract: God does not make contracts with humans. Indeed, according to Edwards, if God were to turn his gaze for even a moment, men and women would fall into the terrible pit of hell:

> So that, thus it is that natural men are held in the hand of God, over the pit of hell; they have deserved the fiery pit, and are already sentenced to it; and God is dreadfully provoked, his anger is as great towards them as to those that are actually suffering the executions of the fierceness of his wrath in hell, and they have done nothing in the least to appease or abate that anger.[42]

Edwards continued to explain that nothing a person does is sufficient to stave off God's wrath. Our actions, whether noble or ignoble, are not enough to save us. Edwards then turned to the matter of practical application:

> The use of this awful subject may be for awakening unconverted persons in this congregation. This that you have heard is the case of every one of you that are out of Christ—the world of misery, that take of burning brimstone, is extended abroad under you. There is the dreadful pit of the glowing flames of the wrath of God; there is hell's wide gaping mouth open; and you have nothing to stand upon, nor any thing to take hold of; there is nothing between you and hell but the air; it is only the power and mere pleasure of God that holds you up.[43]

Finally, Edwards urged the people to reform:

> And let every one that is yet out of Christ, and hanging over the pit of hell, whether they be old men and women, or middle aged, or young people, or little children, now hearken to the loud calls of God's word and providence. This acceptable year of the Lord, a day of such great favor to some, will doubtless be a day of as remarkable

vengeance to others. Men's hearts harden, and their guilt increases apace at such a day as this, if they neglect their souls. . . . Therefore, let every one that is out of Christ, now awake and fly from the wrath to come. The wrath of Almighty God is now undoubtedly hanging over a great part of this congregation. Let every one fly out of Sodom: "Haste and escape for your lives, look not behind you, escape to the mountain, lest you be consumed." [44]

No one in Enfield that day escaped the power of Edwards's eloquence. No one who later read the sermon escaped from it, either. Edwards had proclaimed the awful power and sovereignty of God. He made it plain that there was no hope to be found in good works, good thoughts, or right action. The only possible hope lay in throwing oneself on the immense mercy of God Almighty.

6

The Edwards Home

I am quite willing to live, and quite willing to die;
quite willing to be sick and quite willing to be well; and
quite willing for anything that God will bring upon me!

—Sarah Edwards

M any spiritual leaders live solitary lives or lives that include a minimum of family concerns. This was not the case with Jonathan Edwards, who first grew up in a large family and then had a large family of his own.

One of the keys to understanding his family life is the relationship between Edwards and his wife, Sarah Pierpont Edwards. The eight-year difference in their ages did not have an impact on their marriage; New Englanders married young in those days, and the Edwards-Pierpont union was no exception. What was notable was the extent to which Sarah Edwards's intellectual and religious interests mirrored those of her husband. Both husband and wife were absolutely convinced that the things of this world were a distant second to those of Heaven, and they intended their lives to be examples of righteous behavior.

It could be argued that the Edwards couple was not unusual: Many New England ministers and their wives held this type of belief. The extent to which the Edwardses practiced their faith was unusual, however, and it was made even more challenging by the birth, one by one, of 11 children.

Between 1729 and 1746, Sarah Edwards gave birth to a child virtually every other year. This means that she spent nearly half of her time over the course of 17 years in some stage of pregnancy.

Jonathan Edwards made a careful list of the birth of every child, noting the day, the hour, and the conditions into which each came into the world. The order was as follows: Sarah, Jerusha, Esther, Mary, Lucy, Timothy, Susannah, Eunice, Jonathan, Elizabeth, Pierpont. By a strange coincidence, 6 of the 11 children were born on the Sabbath.[45]

With each new child came immense responsibility and thought. Children were extremely susceptible to disease in those days, and it is truly remarkable that not one of the 11 Edwards children died in infancy. The work of clothing, bathing, and feeding was virtually doubled because of the lack of labor-saving devices. Sarah Edwards had no washing machine, disposable diapers, or electric iron. The daily housework in the Edwards home was accomplished by hand.

THE PASTOR'S WIFE

There is no household diary to record how involved Jonathan Edwards was in the care and the raising of his children, and, given his commitment to the Northampton parish, we can estimate that about 90 percent of the household work was done by Sarah Edwards. She must have been an excellent budgeter of time, and she probably trained her older children to help with the chores. Yet Sarah's responsibilities did not end with caring for her children and managing her household—she was also expected to live up to the social standards set for the wife of the community's pastor.

Every aspect of Sarah Edwards's character was on display, from weekday meetings with other wives to Sunday services when she sat in a front pew, in full view of the congregation. Despite her many responsibilities, Sarah must have managed to balance her responsibilities to her home and her community quite well: Colonial records sing the praises of Sarah Edwards.

Most of the records of Sarah come from the pens of other ministers or ministers-in-training who spent time at the Edwardses' Northampton home. Almost without exception, these letters and notations speak of Sarah Edwards as a remarkable mother, wife, and human being. She ministered to her 11 children, to the many visitors who came, and to her husband, who suffered from chronic indigestion and headaches (not surprising, considering the amount of concentration needed for his work). Only once did Sarah Edwards become overwhelmed by the many roles she had to fulfill, and the records from this brief period indicate that Jonathan Edwards was not only a man of religious conviction, but also of emotional sensitivity.

Jonathan Edwards delivered his famous "Sinners in the Hands of an Angry God" sermon in July 1741. A few months later, Sarah Edwards fell into a deep depression, punctuated by moments and hours of what she described as unbearable giddiness. The death of one her sisters appears to have set off the depression, and Sarah suffered cruelly during the winter of 1741–1742. Suddenly, she lost her grip on the two things that mattered most to her: the welfare of her family and the esteem of the Northampton community. She later described her experience:

> The peace and calm of my mind, and my rest in God, as my only and all sufficient happiness, seemed sensibly above the reach of disturbance from anything but these two: [first] my own good name and fair reputation among men, and especially the esteem and just treatment of the people of this town: [secondly] And, more especially, the esteem and love and kind treatment of my husband.[46]

Sarah's admission of the importance of her husband's opinion, as well as the few letters written between them that have survived, indicate that Jonathan and Sarah Edwards were truly an "interdependent" couple: Each needed the other profoundly. He needed her calm management of the household and her social skill with the neighbors; she needed his inner strength and conviction.

While Jonathan was 70 miles away in Leominster, Massachusetts, Sarah went through several trials and tribulations of her body and soul. She fainted numerous times, appeared to recover, and then fainted again. As one of her most careful biographers has noted, "The beady eye of the modern psychiatrist might spot the phase she entered as a manic one. She thought she was passing through a period of religious ecstasy."[47]

When Edwards returned from Leominster, he ministered to his wife in a direct manner. At a time when the profession had yet been invented, Edwards acted very much like a psychologist. He made Sarah sit and tell him very slowly all the events that preceded her breakdown and then all the feelings that accompanied it. Edwards took careful dictation throughout the talk, and the paper on which he wrote his notes still survives.

Edwards described his wife's experiences in his *A Faithful Narrative*, but he took care to disguise her identity, naming her as one of the townspeople from a good family. Edwards wrote:

> She had a great longing to die, that she might be with Christ, which increased till she thought she did not know how to be patient to wait till God's time should come. But once, when she felt those longings, she thought with herself, "If I long to die, why do I go to physicians?" Whence she concluded that her longings for death were not well regulated. After this she often put it to herself, which she should choose, whether to live or to die, to be sick or to be well; and she found she could not tell, till at last she found herself disposed to say these words: "I am quite willing to live, and quite willing to die; quite willing to be sick, and quite willing to be well; and quite willing for anything that God will bring upon me!"[48]

Whether it was because of her acceptance of fate or from the skillful listening of her husband, Sarah Edwards recovered very well from her winter collapse. The crisis passed.

THE YOUNG MISSIONARY

The spring of 1746 brought a new visitor to the Edwards home, one who would profoundly alter the feelings and thoughts of the family. This was David Brainerd.

Born in Connecticut in 1718, Brainerd came from the same type of pious background that characterized the Edwardses, but he had fewer advantages. He went to Yale College but was expelled early in 1742. The reasons for the expulsion are still uncertain. Full of the spirit of the Great Awakening, Brainerd decided to become a missionary to the Indians, particularly to those of western New York and Pennsylvania.

Brainerd arrived at the Edwards home completely worn out from several years of ardent missionary work. Sarah Edwards noticed his physical condition and summoned a doctor. Brainerd was soon diagnosed as tubercular. Brainerd stayed at the Edwards home, and he became something of a legend to the Edwards children; they saw him as a courageous person who was doing in the flesh what their intellectual father was doing in the spirit.

Jonathan Edwards was very taken by this ardent young man, and in the last months of Brainerd's life, the two men composed Brainerd's biography. Even today, it is difficult to determine how much of the book that resulted is a true chronicle of Brainerd's wanderings and how much was composed by a feverish and tubercular young man, dictating to an older man whom he admired.

Much has been made of the affection between David Brainerd and Jerusha, one of the Edwards daughters. Again, it is unclear whether the nature of the relationship was romantic or if it was more hero worship inspired by Brainerd's missionary activities. In either case, Brainerd died in October 1747 of tuberculosis, and Jerusha Edwards died in February 1748 of the same illness, most likely contracted while she nursed Brainerd.

Jonathan and Sarah Edwards took the loss of Jerusha very hard. Until now they had had the unusual good fortune to see all of their children live. For the first time, the Edwards family experienced the type of misfortune through which they had counseled their neighbors.

Jonathan Edwards's biography of David Brainerd was published in 1747. Although only a marginal seller in its early years, the book was reprinted and reissued many times over the next century. It became the standard account of the life of a missionary in the American wilderness and inspired hundreds of young men at Yale, Harvard, Amherst, and Williams Colleges to become missionaries. Up to the time of the American Civil War (1861–1865), the biography was one of the standard readings for an educated American man.

The biography of Brainerd is difficult to follow because Jonathan Edwards's words and thoughts are hard to separate from those of his subject. Edwards, who had grown up in a family of women and who now lived in a household dominated by female influence, had been delighted to find in Brainerd a man with great spiritual virtues. Edwards's text made much of the trials and sufferings Brainerd exposed himself to, as in the following passage quoted from Brainerd's diary:

> August 14. Spent the day with the Indians. There was one of them who had some time since put away his wife (as is common among them) and taken another woman, and being now brought under some serious impressions, was much concerned about that affair in particular, and seemed fully convinced of the wickedness of that practice and earnestly desirous to know what God would have him do in his present circumstances. When the law of God respecting marriage had been opened to them, and the cause of his leaving his wife inquired into; and when it appeared she had given him no just occasion by unchastity to desert her, and that she was willing to forgive his past misconduct and to live peaceably with him for the future [he] . . . renounced the woman he had last taken and publicly promised to live with and be kind to his wife during life, she also promising the same to him. And here appeared a clear demonstration of the power of God's Word upon their hearts.[49]

Brainerd's experience mirrored Edwards's own in preaching morality and chastity among his parishioners. Edwards's influence, however, was soon to be challenged.

7

A Prophet
Without Honor

A prophet is not without honor save in his own country.

—Matthew 13:57

The first fires of revival had been kindled in Northampton, and perhaps it was too much to hope that they would remain hot for long. By the mid-1740s, Edwards and his family were despondent over the attitude of the people of Northampton toward the matters of God.

THE BAD BOOK

The troubles began early in the 1740s and came to a fever pitch over two matters. The first was the "Bad Book" controversy of 1744. Sometime that year, Edwards learned that some of his younger male congregants had obtained a midwife's manual and were taunting women in town with the information they had read. Edwards saw this offensive behavior as a painful betrayal because some of the men were in their early and mid-20s and therefore had been children during the 1734–1735 revival. It dismayed Edwards that members of his church would behave in such a manner, and he took them to task. He brought them to his parsonage and addressed them directly about their actions but found the young men much less pliable than they had been in the past. One of them, Timothy Root, was heard to say he would not obey a "wig," and that he did not care a bit for Edwards or the secular authorities of Northampton. The reference to a wig was especially painful to Edwards: Ownership of two wigs was about the only indulgence he allowed himself.

Edwards continued to be appalled by the behavior of many young people in the town. They often went to taverns, drank a good deal, and sometimes "bundled" intimately together in the evenings. This behavior was distressing enough on its own, but to know that many of the young people doing this had been his special protégés a decade earlier made it even more painful.

This behavior, shocking to Edwards, is more comprehensible to us today. Thanks to the research of Patricia J. Tracy, we know that Northampton and the Connecticut River Valley as a whole were undergoing social transformations in which it was more and more difficult for young men to obtain land and a home and therefore to marry. Men like Timothy Root saw no need to obey Edwards or the secular authorities if there was no reward system in place for good behavior.

Edwards did not handle the matter well. In a church service in front of the entire congregation, he named all of those who had been involved in the Bad Book incident and asked them to meet with him at his home. Edwards's mistake was in failing to discriminate between the perpetrators and the witnesses, publicly embarrassing many upstanding members of his church. In this single action Edwards lost some of his best supporters.

The Bad Book case was settled with the rendering of private confessions, but in the process, Edwards alienated some of his core parishioners. Making matters worse, Edwards lost his oldest and most trusting patron when Colonel John Stoddard died in 1748.

PARISH POLITICS

Colonel Stoddard, Edwards's uncle and the son of Solomon Stoddard, was the wealthiest and most respected member of the Northampton community. He had been a pillar of strength during Queen Anne's War. This is the American name for part of a larger conflict, primarily between England and France, called the War of Spanish Succession, in which the French tried to expand their power. (The name "War of Spanish Succession" came from Louis XIV's attempt to install his grandson the king of Spain, thus sparking conflict in Europe.) In the end, the French lost much of their Canadian territory to Great Britain. In this conflict, Deerfield, Massachusetts, had been sacked and burned by the French. Later in life, Stoddard was a very successful merchant; he left an estate valued at more than 18,000 pounds sterling. His life bore witness to the transition of Northampton from a frontier town that greatly valued religious conformity to a settled agricultural area in which wealth and titles counted for a great deal more than before.

Stoddard had always been Edwards's most faithful ally. Time and again Stoddard had voiced his support for Edwards's preaching and had therefore kept the squires and leaders of the town behind the minister. Now Stoddard was gone, and Edwards would have to make his way without such assistance.

Even so, Edwards might have continued without trouble had he not insisted on changing a cardinal rule of the Northampton church. He wanted to reverse the long-standing policy of

THE LOUISBOURG EXPEDITION OF 1745

Religious and spiritual leaders generally are little interested in military events. Edwards, however, raised in a Calvinist tradition, saw every victory for Anglo America over the Catholic French as further evidence of God's favor.

King George's War (known in Europe as the War of Austrian Succession), between England and France, began in 1744. In the late winter of 1745, the Massachusetts Provincial Government decided to send a fleet and army to capture Louisbourg, the French fortress on Cape Breton Island at the top of Nova Scotia. More than 20 men from Northampton participated in the siege; one was Major Seth Pomeroy, whose journal of the siege provides one of the best descriptions available for eighteenth-century siege warfare.

Louisbourg was seen as the greatest fortified place in North America, but the New England farmers and fishermen took it in a siege that lasted only about 40 days. When the news came to Boston and Northampton, the New Englanders were ecstatic.

Edwards was thrilled to learn that Louisbourg had fallen. Like Major Pomeroy and many other New Englanders, Edwards believed this was a visible sign of victory in the ongoing war against popery (or Papism). Just one year later, in 1746, Edwards had another reason to rejoice when he learned that the Scottish forces of "Bonnie Prince Charlie" (Prince Charles Edward Stuart, also known as the Young Pretender) had been defeated at the Battle of Culloden. King James II, a Catholic, had been deposed by his mostly Protestant subjects. The prince, James II's grandson, had invaded England with a small army in order to reestablish his family's rule. Without the support promised by England and France, however, he had to retreat and was soundly defeated at Culloden Moor. Edwards had long kept up an active correspondence with Scottish ministers, and now he rejoiced in their victory over the forces of Catholicism.

half-way admission to the church and full admission to the Lord's Supper, commonly known as Communion.

Solomon Stoddard, the colonel's father, had begun the policy of open admission to communion as early as 1680. By 1748, when his son Colonel Stoddard died, the policy had been in place in the community for almost 70 years. Edwards now decided that too many people had been admitted to full church membership during the two awakenings of 1734 and 1740 and that there needed to be a stricter policy of examination for new members.

The trickiest part was choosing who would decide what was and was not a legitimate act of saving grace. It seems that the Reverend Edwards believed he was the only member of the parish who had the experience and knowledge to perform such a task.

The storm broke over this matter. Very few of the Northampton congregants believed in the policy for admission that preceded Stoddard's, and even fewer believed that one man could make the choices necessary.

In the past, Edwards might have received help from Colonel Stoddard and therefore from the other village squires. Since Stoddard's death, however, the town squires had turned against Edwards. Some of them were emboldened by a long list of grievances drawn up by Edwards's cousin Joseph Hawley. During the spiritual revival Edwards had led in Northampton in 1735, it was Hawley's father who reflected on what he considered to be the sorry state of his soul and committed suicide. Hawley repeatedly claimed that he did not blame the Reverend Edwards for his father's suicide. Instead, Hawley insisted that his opposition was based on Edwards becoming too dictatorial in his ministry.

A keener politician would have seen the way the wind was blowing and adjusted his sails accordingly. Edwards, though, had always disdained seeking favor from the crowd.

Something seems to have broken within Jonathan Edwards in 1749 and 1750. He would probably say the opposite, that his will had become firmer and that he could no longer bear the contradictions of his ministry. In retrospect, however, it seems as if Edwards was determined to sabotage his ministry. Perhaps he was weary of the duties of a country parson or perhaps he wanted to go elsewhere. In either case, he pushed ahead with his controversial attempt to change the church policy.

Popular resistance rose at once. Edwards's parishioners were accustomed to almost three generations of the Stoddard method and they would not let Stoddard's grandson change the rules on them. Calls were made within the parish for Edwards to be removed. Typical to his nature, Edwards responded in a calm manner and referred the matter to a general council of ministers.

In the spring of 1750, the Hampshire County council of ministers gathered to discuss whether to dismiss Edwards. In the past, Edwards had been able to obtain the backing of the council, but his cousin Israel Williams, who may have "had it in" for Edwards, now had greater influence. The final vote, cast in June, came to 9 votes in favor and 10 against. Not only was Edwards estranged from his Northampton congregants, he also was now distanced from his ministerial colleagues.

The First Church of Northampton dismissed Edwards on June 22, 1750. After 23 years in the pulpit, he was exiled by his own parishioners. Edwards had one last opportunity to speak up. In his farewell sermon, he preached:

> The Apostle, in the preceding part of the chapter, declares what great troubles he met with, in the course of his ministry. In the text, and two foregoing verses, he declares what were his comforts and supports under the troubles he met with. There are four things in particular.
>
> 1. That he had approved himself to his own conscience. . . .
>
> 2. Another thing he speaks of as matter of comfort, is, that as he had approved himself to his own conscience so he had also to the consciences of his hearers, the Corinthians to whom he now wrote, and that they should approve him at the day of judgment.

3. The hope he had of seeing the blessed fruit of his labours and sufferings in the ministry, in their happiness and glory in that great day of accounts.

4. That in his ministry among the Corinthians, he had approved himself to his Judge, who would approve and reward his faithfulness in that day.[50]

Edwards went on at great length. Several times in the sermon he addressed the younger members of his congregation:

Since I have been settled in the work of the ministry, in this place, I have ever had a peculiar concern for the souls of the young people, and a desire that religion might flourish among them; and have especially exerted myself in order to it; because I knew the special opportunity they had beyond others, and that ordinarily those, whom God intended mercy for, were brought to fear and love him in their youth. . . . And so far as I know my heart, it was from thence that I formerly led this church to some measure, for the suppressing of vice among our young people, which gave so great offense, and by which I became so obnoxious.[51]

It must have been with a heavy heart that Edwards concluded. His mission in Northampton was over.

8

Mission to
the Indians

We haven't reason at all to dispair.

—Jonathan Edwards, on his belief that God
would strike down the forces of Roman Papacy

E dwards's next step was influenced by his friendship with David Brainerd. Edwards had a great admiration for this young man and perhaps a desire to emulate him. After he was ejected from his pulpit in June 1750, Edwards had the opportunity to strike out as a missionary. The only question was where to go.

A NEW LIFE IN STOCKBRIDGE

Over the previous decade, Edwards had corresponded with a number of prominent ministers in Scotland. These letters from across the Atlantic had persuaded Edwards that the Scottish people would be more receptive to true church reformation than the Anglo Americans were. To move across the Atlantic at the age of 46 seemed too great a task, however, and Edwards decided to become a missionary to the Native Americans of Stockbridge, Massachusetts.

Located in the southwest corner of the Massachusetts colony, Stockbridge was only about 50 miles from Northampton. The difference of those 50 miles, however, meant a great deal of change. Northampton was a well-settled and well-established community, whereas Stockbridge was truly on the frontier. Edwards was eager to move to Stockbridge, but his family was less willing: His wife and children stayed behind while he went to Stockbridge in the winter of 1751. By the time he returned in the spring, he had resolved on the move.

Esther Edwards, the third of the children, had long been a vivacious and discerning girl. Now, at the age of 20, she was engaged to marry the Reverend Aaron Burr of New Jersey. He was an ardent New Light supporter of Edwards and had come north to Northampton specifically to visit the family. Whether or not he knew of Esther's charms before he visited the Edwardses, he became completely enamored with her after his arrival, and their marriage was arranged within a few days' time.

Edwards did not regret the loss of his daughter to a man like Burr. Indeed, Esther's marriage may have made things somewhat easier for Edwards as he planned the move to Stockbridge. Still, there was some sadness in the Edwards family as a whole. Beloved Jerusha had died a few years ago, and Esther was now married and about to leave. The entire Edwards family was, if not breaking up, at least beginning to fray at the edges.

FAMILY FEUDS

The remaining Edwardses were in Stockbridge by the early part of 1752. They soon found that they had not escaped the quarrels with relatives that they had known in Northampton. The Stoddard-Williams clan was so large and dominant in western Massachusetts that there was a whole branch already in Stockbridge. Foremost among them were Colonel Ephraim Williams and his two children, Ephraim, Jr., and Abigail.

Though the colonel and his son could be considered imposing, Jonathan Edwards and his family found 25-year-old Abigail even more formidable. She had been married twice, first to John Sergeant, who started the mission to the Mohicans, and then, after Sergeant's death, to Brigadier General Joseph Dwight. Both men appear to have been completely devoted to her, and Abigail used her influence to make life very difficult for her Edwards relatives.

There is no definitive explanation for the poor relationship that existed between the Edwards and the Williams families, but one speculation is that the bad blood began with a fight between Jonathan Edwards's mother and one of her siblings. Whether or not this was true, by the time the Edwards clan left Northampton, there were very few Williamses with whom they could have a pleasant conversation. As usual, Jonathan Edwards hunkered down in his study, with his books, leaving Sarah and the children to deal with the fluctuating family relations.

Edwards was consumed with his new task. Throughout his career, he had preached to people who were already converted or to people familiar with his manner of preaching. For the first time, he had an audience to whom the Bible and Christianity were new, and he made the most of the situation. Some of his family members entered the Mohican world with equal enthusiasm. Jonathan, Jr., later recalled being so immersed in his new environment during his years in Stockbridge that he thought in the language of the local Native Americans.

There is a sense that Jonathan Edwards was slipping, both as a parent and as a minister. He still loved his children deeply, but the loss of his beloved daughter Jerusha, followed by the loss of his Northampton pulpit, had done something to him inside, and he was less available to his large family. Meanwhile, he continued to experience difficulties with his relatives in Stockbridge.

Because of the marriage of Abigail Williams and General Dwight, Jonathan Edwards had to fight for every inch of ground in Stockbridge. The money for the mission to the Indians came from charitable sources in England, which was so far away that disputes took a year or more to resolve. Others in Stockbridge noticed the increasing bitterness between the Edwards and Williams families; the Edwardses were not even invited to a prominent Williams wedding.

Finally, a set of instructions to resolve the tensions between the Edwardses and Williamses came from the leaders of the missionary movement in London. Jonathan Edwards was to run the school for the Mohawk and Mohican children and the Williamses were to stay out of the matter. Edwards found this a hollow triumph, for many of the Indian students had seen enough of the fighting between their white teachers and pulled out during the winter of 1753. As Edwards biographer George Marsden wrote, "The events that led to the disaffection of many of the Indians who had spent time at Stockbridge illustrate the great defect in English missions to the Native Americans and why they were so much less successful than their French counterparts."[52] The English-American settlers were constantly spilling into settlements like Stockbridge, swallowing up large areas of land. Contrast this with the behavior of a handful of French Jesuit priests who went to convert the Huron in the wilderness, and it is easy to see why the French succeeded more often than the English. Land and the desire to own it almost always drove a wedge between the Anglo Americans and their Native-American Indian friends.

Things were about to become much worse. In 1753, two Stockbridge Native-American Indians attempted to stop two Anglo Americans who they believed were attempting to steal horses. The English fired on the Indians, killing one of them. The soldiers were taken to Springfield for trial; one was found innocent and the other was found guilty of manslaughter. These verdicts did not satisfy the Mohicans, who began to desert Stockbridge in increasing numbers. There was even talk of an Indian raid planned for future revenge.

Edwards was deeply distressed by both the verdicts and the effect on his congregation. Things had reached such a low point that his school dwindled to about six students, two of whom he boarded in his home. At the same time, however, he showed remarkable faith in the evangelistic process: He sent his son Jonathan, Jr., on a missionary trip to the Susquehannock River.

THE FRENCH AND INDIAN WAR

In the late summer of 1754, the Edwardses learned that a new war had commenced. A young Virginia colonel named George Washington had fought the first two skirmishes of what became known as the French and Indian War. (This was part of a larger war fought on three continents called the Seven Years' War, which grew out of previously existing conflicts among many European nations, chiefly England and France.) Although he won the first skirmish, Washington was trapped at a log fort called Fort Necessity and was forced to surrender in July 1754. The war had begun on an ominous note.

For the British people, the war was generally seen as a continuation of their many conflicts with the French. But to the people of New England, and to fervent Puritans like Jonathan Edwards, the French and Indian War was larger and even more frightening: it was the culmination of a long battle between the Puritans of New England and the Papists (Roman Catholics) of French Canada.

One year after George Washington's defeat in Pennsylvania, in the spring of 1755, British General Edward Braddock arrived with two regiments of troops. Braddock, guided by Colonel Washington, began a long march through Maryland and Pennsylvania on his way toward Fort Duquesne, a French fort located where Pittsburgh, Pennsylvania, is today. Braddock came within eight miles of the fort when he and his regiment were attacked, surrounded, and killed. About two-thirds of the British officers were killed in a battle that indicated a French ascendancy in America.

This terrible news affected nearly all Anglo Americans. Esther Edwards Burr, safe at Princeton, feared for her father and her family in Stockbridge. Edwards, as was usually the case, took the news calmly. He delivered a sermon on the events, noting that "we haven't reason at all to despair." [53] Edwards was a firm believer in the divine plan for America and the world as a whole: If God was now building up the forces of Roman Papacy in America (as the majority of French were members of the Roman Catholic Church), God would cast them down to even greater triumph in the future. To keep his spirits up, Edwards kept a log of all the evil events that happened to the Papal cause throughout the world. When British ships captured or defeated French forces, Edwards noted the ship names, number of cannons, and number of men. He was determined to keep gloomy thoughts at bay.

A more mixed batch of news came in September 1755. Edwards learned that a combined force of British and Indians had won a partial victory at the Battle of Lake George, in New York, fought in early September. The bad news was that the British and colonists suffered many losses, including Ephraim Williams, Jr., and one of the Hawley cousins. Even worse, Chief Hendrick of the Mohawks was killed. He had been the most important ally of the British and colonists, and many people feared that the Mohawk tribe might turn against the Anglo-American cause.

In the crisis and panic that followed, hundreds of militiamen descended on Stockbridge for a few days. The Edwardses' diaries

A major figure in the First Great Awakening, Jonathan Edwards is considered by many to be the greatest theologian in American history. He remains one of the most respected men of the Colonial period for being not only a man of great religious conviction, but also of great ideas, and he conveyed both through his sermons. His "Sinners in the Hands of an Angry God" persists as being one of his most well-known works.

This page from Edwards's graduation oration at Yale is written in Classical Latin, the language of the learned during his time. Edwards performed his oration in 1723, a critical time in the Yale's history: just a year earlier, the Reverend Timothy Cutler and a few other instructors from the college announced that they had converted to the Anglican church. Edwards's speech was crucial in reasserting Yale's Congregational heritage.

John Calvin published his influential *Institutes of the Christian Religion* in 1536. One of the main principles of his work is God's all-knowing and all-powerful nature. When Edwards had his spiritual breakthrough at the age of 20, he came to understand Calvin's theology.

Edwards was inspired by the Enlightenment philosopher John Locke. Locke's ideas shaped much of eighteenth-century thought, focusing on scientific matters and the rational human mind. Edwards, unlike some religious leaders of his time, believed that there was room for both science and religion, and that the two did not necessarily conflict with each other. He wanted to be as influential an author as Locke.

F

Although George Whitefield was an Anglican, he was such a powerful public speaker that Edwards invited him into the Edwards home and joined him at evangelical functions in New England when Whitefield conducted a tour of America in 1740. Through Whitefield's journals of his time at the Edwards home, we have a first-hand account of the piety of the family.

David Brainerd, preaching to a Native-American tribe in this drawing, inspired Edwards to perform missionary work after he was relieved of his duties as pastor to the Northampton Congregation. Brainerd and Edwards developed a close relationship when the young missionary came to stay at the Edwards home when he was sick with tuberculosis. Edwards used Brainerd's journals to write a biography of the young man's time with the Native Americans.

hold no record of this, but the family submitted a request to the Massachusetts legislature for reimbursement for 850 meals served to militiamen during the week. Such a crowd must have placed a great strain on the Edwards family.

Edwards needed all his effort to keep up his spirits over the next two years. In 1756, the French captured Fort Oswego, on the eastern side of Lake Ontario. This was 300 miles from

CHIEF HENDRICK

Chief Hendrick was the son of a Mohican father and a Mohawk mother. Because the Mohawk Indians traced their lineage through the mother's side of the family, Hendrick became an important Mohawk chief.

Born around 1680, Hendrick went to England in 1711 and 1740. His portrait was painted both times, and he became something of a celebrity at the English court. Hendrick was the most faithful ally the Anglo Americans had among the Mohawk Indians, but he also took the liberty to admonish them at times. In 1754, he lectured an Anglo delegation at Albany, New York: "Look at the French, they are men, they are fortifying—but we are ashamed to say it, you are like women bare and open without any fortifications."* From this conference came Benjamin Franklin's famous political cartoon that showed the different English colonies as part of a disembodied snake. The caption read, "Unite or Die."

In the summer of 1755, Hendrick brought several hundred warriors to join the Anglo Americans at the foot of Lake George. When the Anglo Americans learned that the French enemy was in the neighborhood, Hendrick was asked to lead a column of men to reconnoiter. He protested, saying, "If it comes to fight, too few, if they die, too many." Like a brave ally, however, he led his men forth. They were ambushed, and Hendrick was killed early in the fighting.

Although William Johnson of New York won credit for the victory and was named Sir William Johnson as a result, Chief Hendrick was an important factor in the campaign. Never again, in either the French and Indian War or the American Revolution, would the Anglo Americans have such a good friend.

*Mark Carnes and John Garraty, *American National Biography*, vol. 10. New York: Oxford University Press, 1999, p. 581.

Stockbridge, but Edwards and others feared what might happen to their settlement.

In 1757, the French struck again. The Marquis de Montcalm brought about 8,000 French and Indian troops south from Montreal. He landed at the base of Lake George and captured Fort William Henry after a siege. New Englanders dreaded an invasion by the French, but Montcalm turned his army around after taking Fort William Henry, and western Massachusetts was spared.

By September 1757, Edwards and his family may have been on the edge of despair. Three years of warfare had produced mostly defeats for the English. The French appeared ready to attack and plunder the entire Anglo-American frontier, including Stockbridge. Then, at the worst of times, the Edwardses learned of another important loss. The Reverend Aaron Burr, Edwards's son-in-law, collapsed and died from overwork. Esther Edwards was now a widow with two young children.

9

A Ray of Light and a Dark Cloud

A holy and good God has covered us with a dark cloud.

—Sarah Edwards, letter to Esther Edwards Burr

Throughout his life, Jonathan Edwards had been as much a scholar as a preacher. He had always preferred his library to pastoral counseling, and now, in the autumn of 1757, a new opportunity beckoned to him. He had lost a wonderful son-in-law, but he was now offered the position of president of the new College of New Jersey.

A NEW OPPORTUNITY

Aaron Burr, Sr., (the father of Esther Edwards's deceased husband) had been the second president of the college; Edwards now had the chance to become the third. He did not immediately jump at the possibility, because he had changed locations twice and had been disappointed by the results. On October 19, Edwards wrote to the college trustees:

> Rev. and Hon. Gentlemen,
>
> I was not a little surprised, on receiving the unexpected notice, of your having made choice of me, to succeed the late President Burr, as the Head of Nassau Hall.—I am much in doubt, whether I am called to undertake the business, which you have done me the unmerited honor to choose me for.—If some regard may be had to my outward comfort, I might mention the many inconveniencies, and great detriment, which may be sustained, by my removing, with my numerous family, so far from all the estate I have in the world (without any prospect of disposing of it, under present circumstances, but with great loss,) now when we have scarcely got over the trouble and damage, sustained by our removal from Northampton.[54]

Edwards explained that the material circumstances were not the foremost problem:

> I have a constitution, in many respects peculiarly unhappy, attended with flaccid solids, vapid, sizy and scarce fluids, and a low tide of spirits. . . . This makes me shrink at the thoughts of taking upon me, in the decline of life, such a new and

great business, attended with such a multiplicity of cares, and requiring such a degree of activity, alertness, and spirit of government; especially as succeeding one so remarkably well qualified in these respects.[55]

Edwards also expressed that he had not made a general study of mathematics in many years, another reason for his unsuitability as president of a college. A reader might wonder whether Edwards was trying to make the trustees "raise the ante" in some way to induce him to accept. It is likely, however, that Edwards truly saw himself as unfit for such a post. He was a scholar and a man of letters but had never been successful as an administrator. Why would the trustees want a man who had been ejected from his own pulpit seven years ago?

The trustees would not take no for an answer. They continued to send letters, urging Edwards to accept the post. By late November 1747, he had decided to accept the position and move to New Jersey. Esther Edwards Burr was delighted. She had lost her husband but now knew that her parents and some of her siblings would come to live with her.

Jonathan Edwards arrived at Princeton early in 1758. He had hardly set up his first meeting with the trustees when he received the news of his father's death. Timothy Edwards had been in good health throughout most of his 89 years. Jonathan Edwards accepted this loss as one of the worst in a decade in which he had known plenty of sorrow. His daughter Jerusha, his friend David Brainerd, his son-in-law Aaron Burr, and now his father were all dead. Edwards was preoccupied with thoughts of his own death. He often wrote to his children to this effect, reminding them of how fleeting life was and of the great need to find safety in the Lord before their demise.

FAMILY TRAGEDY

Smallpox was prevalent in New Jersey during the late winter of 1758. The French and Indian War, with its movements of troops and population, may have contributed to the disease's spread that year. Soon after arriving in Princeton, Jonathan Edwards considered whether he needed an inoculation for the smallpox (to learn more about this disease, enter the keywords "smallpox facts" into any Internet search engine and browse the listed websites).

Inoculation is not quite the same as vaccination. Inoculation is a dangerous process in which the illness is injected into the subject's body so the body can develop immunity to the disease. When it worked, the inoculation provided a lifetime of freedom

AARON BURR, JR.

One of the great historical anomalies is that the worst scoundrel of early American politics was the grandson of America's greatest theologian. Aaron Burr, Jr., grandson of Jonathan Edwards, served as vice president of the United States between 1801 and 1805. His heritage, though, is not what made him so famous: He shot and killed Alexander Hamilton in the most famous of all American duels.

Aaron Burr, Sr., died in 1757. The smallpox epidemic of 1758 killed Jonathan Edwards and Esther Edwards Burr, and Sarah Edwards died of dysentery later that same year. In the space of 12 months, two-year-old Aaron Burr, Jr., lost both of his parents and both of his maternal grandparents. He was raised by uncles and cousins, none of whom devoted much time to their young charge.

When the American Revolution began in 1775, Aaron Burr joined the Patriot cause. He served under Benedict Arnold in the heroic march to Quebec City and later was a colonel in the Continental Army. Burr served with distinction during the war; only after its conclusion in 1783 did he begin to show the traits—deceit and ruthlessness—that made him the subject of anger and scorn.

In 1800, Burr ran for president. He tied with Thomas Jefferson in the electoral college and then lost the run-off election in the U.S. House of Representatives. Under the curious rules of that time, Burr, as the runner-up, served as Jefferson's vice president. Toward the end of his term, Burr challenged Hamilton to a duel and killed him on the west side of the Hudson River.

Burr later was arrested and tried for treason. He was acquitted and left the country for a number of years. He returned in the early 1830s and made trouble in his old age. Just one year before his death, he was sued for divorce on the grounds of adultery.

from the disease. Vaccination, which became available about 40 years later, is a much safer process with a very short recuperation period. Edwards knew that many people feared inoculation, and he may have decided to be inoculated as a public statement. He was always a believer in the progress of science, which he saw as accompanying the progress of Christianity throughout the world.

Edwards and his daughter Esther received the inoculation from Doctor William Shippen on February 23, 1758. (Sarah Edwards and the other family members were still in Stockbridge.)

All seemed fine for the first few days, but Edwards then took a turn for the worse. He became feverish, and the spots from the pox did not disappear but rather grew. It became apparent he had received too large a dose of the inoculation and that his body was succumbing to the disease.

Edwards was calm during the last days of his life. He had long ago accepted that he had a weak constitution, and it was not shocking that he contracted smallpox from the risky inoculation. Nevertheless, he must have grieved for his family. He still had several young children; he would have to trust his beloved wife to take care of them.

Toward the end of his suffering, Edwards called in his daughter Lucy. He reportedly said to her:

> Dear Lucy, it seems to me to be the will of God that I must shortly leave you; therefore give my kindest love to my dear wife, and tell her, that the uncommon union, which has so long subsisted between us, has been of such a nature, as I trust is spiritual, and therefore will continue forever: and I hope she will be supported under so great a trial, and submit cheerfully to the will of God. And as to my children, you are now like to be left fatherless, which I hope will be an inducement to you all to seek a Father, who will never fail you. And as to my funeral, I would have it be like Mr. Burr's; and any additional sum of money that might be expected to be laid out that was, I would have it disposed of to charitable uses.[56]

Edwards died on March 22, 1758.

Doctor Shippen immediately wrote to Sarah Edwards, assuring her that her husband had been peaceful throughout his illness. Sarah instantly made preparations to go to New Jersey. Esther would need her mother more than ever, especially with two small children in the house.

Sarah Edwards wrote to Esther, telling her she would come quickly:

> O my very dear child,
>
> What shall I say. A holy and good God has covered us with dark cloud. O that we may all kiss the rod and lay our hands on our mouthes [sic]. The Lord has done it. He has made me adore his goodness that we had him so long. But my God lives and he has my heart. O what a legacy my husband and your father has left us. We are all given to God and there I am and love to be.[57]

By the time this letter arrived in Princeton, Esther Edwards Burr was already dead. She fell to the same inoculation for the smallpox that had killed her father.

Sarah Edwards set out for New Jersey. She went to Philadelphia, where she fell ill with dysentery and died early in October 1758. Her body was taken to Princeton, and the four family members—Aaron Burr, Sr., Jonathan Edwards, Esther Burr, and Sarah Edwards—were all buried together.

10

Jonathan Edwards's Legacy

Edwards was infinitely more than a theologian. He was one of America's five or six major artists, who happened to work with ideas instead of with poems or novels.

—Perry Miller, Edwards biographer

H istorians use many criteria to evaluate the lives of men and women, examining first what people accomplished during their lifetimes, and then the influence they had on later generations. This is especially the case with Jonathan Edwards, who is still considered one of the greatest theologians America has ever produced.

AN EDWARDS REVIVAL

By 1940, it appeared that scholars had made up their mind about Edwards, ultimately deciding that though he was an important man, his mission had failed. Then came Perry Miller.

It has been argued that no one in the twentieth century understood the seventeenth- and eighteenth-century Puritans better than Perry Miller. His magnificent book *The New England Mind* remains the critical work in the field. Miller probed the Puritan soul and found it fascinating as well as repellant (It should be added that Miller had the same reactions to himself; see sidebar).

Miller described Edwards as one of the native geniuses or artists:

> The truth is, Edwards was infinitely more than a theologian. He was one of America's five or six major artists, who happened to work with ideas instead of with poems or novels. He was much more a psychologist and a poet than a logician, and though he devoted his genius to topics derived from the body of divinity—the will, virtue, sin—he treated them in the manner of the very finest speculators, in the manner of Augustine, Aquinas, and Pascal, as problems not of dogma but of life. . . . If the student penetrates behind the technical language, he discovers an intelligence which, as much as Emerson's, Melville's, or Mark Twain's, is both an index of American society and a comment upon it.[58]

For Perry Miller, Edwards was one of the modern American thinkers. Virtually every scholar who has read Miller's work has come away with the impression that Edwards belonged as much to the tumultuous twentieth century as to the eighteenth.

SOCIAL HISTORY

Thirty years after Miller, Patricia J. Tracy published her own theories on Edwards. Schooled in the new social history of the 1970s, Tracy applied painstaking methods of social science to Edwards's Northampton years in her book *Jonathan Edwards, Pastor*. Tracy may not have been the first historian to notice the coincidence between the Northampton revival of 1734 and the shortage of new farmland in the Northampton area, but she was the first to put those facts into a framework acceptable to social scientists. She stated her case:

PERRY MILLER

Perry Miller has been credited with making the Puritans and Yankees real for twentieth-century Americans.

Born in Chicago in 1905, Miller spent time as a part-time actor and as a merchant sailor before turning to the study of history. He and his wife moved to Cambridge, Massachusetts, in 1930, and he took up his studies of the Puritans and Yankees, interrupted only by honorable service in the U.S. military during World War II. Although he was a self-professed atheist, Miller penetrated deeper into the Puritan mind-set than did any of his contemporaries. He published *Orthodoxy in Massachusetts* (1933), *The New England Mind: The Seventeenth Century* (1939), and *The New England Mind: From Colony to Province* (1953), along with his monumental *Jonathan Edwards* (1949).

Miller did not necessarily relish or even like the Puritans and Yankees. He saw in them, however, the germ of the American mind and soul. Whatever was done and thought in the seventeenth and eighteenth centuries, in New England especially, had great relevance in the present.

Miller died in Cambridge in December 1963, just weeks after the assassination of President John F. Kennedy, which had thrown him into deep despair. For Miller, men like Kennedy resembled the better part of the American spirit, which derived its light and its darkness from the Puritan and Yankee past.

Much of the modern psychoanalytical literature on conversion experiences points to the commonness of a crisis in late adolescence, as the individual must make a transition between the social status of child and that of adult by accepting certain economic responsibilities and by finding a comfortable new position vis-à-vis parental authority. Empirical research done in the late nineteenth century found a strong pattern of adolescent conversion, and most twentieth century psychological theory accepts the universality of a crisis in adolescence. Although we do not know how much of that turmoil was present in pre-industrial societies, the frequency with which contemporaries remarked on the importance of adolescent constituencies for revival preachers in the 1730s and 1740s tells us that there was a crisis of adolescence in that era, also.[59]

Tracy's thesis was that the young people of Northampton were especially receptive to Edwards's message when they first heard it around 1734 and 1735 but that these same people were quick to reject his leadership a decade or so later. During those intervening 10 to 12 years, they had met and overcome their youth crises and were now able to function in the world without this benevolent pastor, who felt so betrayed by their rejection.

From the social science standpoint, Tracy's admirable work was the final word. Lacking more evidence of the social structure of 1730s Northampton, it was impossible to investigate the matter further. Tracy's book remains one of the most important in the field, and her path-breaking method of research opened the way for similar studies of the Great Awakening as a whole.

What about Jonathan Edwards the man? Was he more than the individual roles of pastor, father, son, missionary, and college president? Was there some overarching identity that encompassed all these subidentities?

A CONTEMPORARY LOOK

George Marsden's *Jonathan Edwards* answered these questions when it was published in 2003. A historian at Notre Dame, Marsden, unlike Perry Miller, was a quiet, unobtrusive man who pursued his subject with unrelenting determination. The result was the finest and most comprehensive study of Edwards to date. No scholar had come so close to Edwards the man and portrayed him as such.

Like biographers before him, Marsden made much of Jonathan Edwards's early years. Marsden pointed to the powerful influence of the Reverend Timothy Edwards but also clearly demonstrated that Jonathan grew up in a world of women, surrounded by his mother and sisters. More than any previous historian, Marsden dug into and highlighted the rather painful details of Edwards's paternal grand-mother's insanity. He hinted that this pathological streak in the family brought a counterreaction first from Timothy Edwards and then from his son.

Marsden concluded by giving Edwards his due both as a man of the Enlightenment and of the devotion to religious matters:

> Edwards thus addressed one of the greatest mysteries facing traditional theism in the post-Newtonian universe: how can the creator of such an unimaginably vast universe be in intimate communication with creatures so infinitely inferior to himself? How can it be that God hears their prayers and responds by caring not only about their eternal souls but even about the details of their temporal lives? To answer such questions one would have to face more starkly than is usually done the immensity of the distance between God and human and between God's ways and our understandings. At the same time, Edwards insisted, if God is meaningfully related to us, God must be intimately involved with the governance of all the universe in its detail. Further, God must be governing it in some way that also grants the maximum possible autonomy to created beings. Whether Edwards, or anyone else, adequately explains how this mystery may be resolved is a matter of some debate.[60]

THE FINAL WORD

What more can be said of Jonathan Edwards?

First, he was a man of God. Blessed as he was with a remarkable wife and 11 children, they always came second to his relationship with God. Edwards's primary duty, as he saw it, was to hear the word of God and to interpret it for others.

Second, he was a man of tradition. Many Americans prided themselves on having broken away from their family of origin and therefore being able to remake themselves. This was not the case with Edwards. Whether he was in Northampton, in Stockbridge, at Yale, or at the College of New Jersey, he was always very much the son of Timothy Edwards and Esther Stoddard.

Third, he was a man who believed in books. America has produced no pastor since with such a love for learning. Edwards was probably the best-read American of his lifetime.

Fourth, and probably most important in his eyes, Edwards was a man who believed in the covenant of the New Englanders with God. Only the pure of heart shall see God, the Bible tells us, and Edwards probably would have limited that to the pure of mind as well. Edwards firmly believed that, in time, the Antichrist, which he saw as the Roman Catholic faith, would be overthrown and the Puritan saints would triumph.

Last, he was a man of extraordinary single-mindedness. There were few contradictions in his character or his behavior. Not even his harshest critics suggested that he shirked his duty or tried to avoid hardship. Edwards underwent many hardships and pains in his quest for God and God's truth.

We are left with a man who was true to himself, loving toward his family, and forgiving toward his many foes. He was the finest representative of the Puritan spirit in America, and his legacy lives with us today.

APPENDIX

APPENDIX

SINNERS IN THE HANDS OF AN ANGRY GOD

Enfield, Connecticut
July 8, 1741

> *"Their foot shall slide in due time."*
>
> Deuteronomy 32:35

In this verse is threatened the vengeance of God on the wicked unbelieving Israelites, who were God's visible people, and who lived under the means of grace; but who, notwithstanding all God's wonderful works towards them, remained (as verse 28) void of counsel, having no understanding in them. Under all the cultivations of heaven, they brought forth bitter and poisonous fruit; as in the two verses next preceding the text.— The expression I have chosen for my text, *their foot shall slide in due time*, seems to imply the following things, relating to the punishment and destruction to which these wicked Israelites were exposed.

1. That they were always exposed to *destruction*; as one that stands or walks in slippery places is always exposed to fall. This is implied in the manner of their destruction coming upon them, being represented by their foot sliding. The same is expressed, Psalm 72:18: *"Surely thou didst set them in slippery places; thou castedst them down into destruction."*

2. It implies, that they were always exposed to *sudden unexpected* destruction. As he that walks in slippery places is every moment liable to fall, he cannot foresee one moment whether he shall stand or fall the next; and when he does fall, he falls at once without warning: Which is also expressed in Psalm 73:18–19. *"Surely thou didst set them in slippery places; thou castedst them down into destruction: How are they brought into desolation as in a moment!"*

3. Another thing implied is, that they are liable to fall *of themselves*, without being thrown down by the hand of another; as he that stands or walks on slippery ground needs nothing but his own weight to throw him down.

4. That the reason why they are not fallen already and do not fall now is only that God's appointed time is not come. For it is said, that when that due time, or appointed time comes, *their foot shall slide.* Then they shall be left to fall, as they are inclined by their own weight. God will not hold them up in these slippery places any longer, but will let them go; and then, at that very instant, they shall fall into destruction; as he that stands on such slippery declining ground, on the edge of a pit, he cannot stand alone, when he is let go he immediately falls and is lost.

The observation from the words that I would now insist upon is this.—"There is nothing that keeps wicked men at any one moment out of hell, but the mere pleasure of God."—By the *mere* pleasure of God, I mean his *sovereign* pleasure, his arbitrary will, restrained by no obligation, hindered by no manner of difficulty, any more than if nothing else but God's mere will had in the least degree, or in any respect whatsoever, any hand in the preservation of wicked men one moment.— The truth of this observation may appear by the following considerations.

1. There is no want of *power* in God to cast wicked men into hell at any moment. Men's hands cannot be strong when God rises up. The strongest have no power to resist him, nor can any deliver out of his hands.—He is not only able to cast wicked men into hell, but he can most easily do it. Sometimes an earthly prince meets with a great deal of difficulty to

subdue a rebel, who has found means to fortify himself, and has made himself strong by the numbers of his followers. But it is not so with God. There is no fortress that is any defence from the power of God. Though hand join in hand, and vast multitudes of God's enemies combine and associate themselves, they are easily broken in pieces. They are as great heaps of light chaff before the whirlwind; or large quantities of dry stubble before devouring flames. We find it easy to tread on and crush a worm that we see crawling on the earth; so it is easy for us to cut or singe a slender thread that any thing hangs by: thus easy is it for God, when he pleases, to cast his enemies down to hell. What are we, that we should think to stand before him, at whose rebuke the earth trembles, and before whom the rocks are thrown down?

2. They *deserve* to be cast into hell; so that divine justice never stands in the way, it makes no objection against God's using his power at any moment to destroy them. Yea, on the contrary, justice calls aloud for an infinite punishment of their sins. Divine justice says of the tree that brings forth such grapes of Sodom, "*Cut it down, why cumbereth it the ground?*" Luke 13:7. The sword of divine justice is every moment brandished over their heads, and it is nothing but the hand of arbitrary mercy, and God's mere will, that holds it back.

3. They are already under a sentence of *condemnation* to hell. They do not only justly deserve to be cast down thither, but the sentence of the law of God, that eternal and immutable rule of righteousness that God has fixed between him and mankind, is gone out against them, and stands against them; so

that they are bound over already to hell. John 3:18. "*He that believeth not is condemned already.*" So that every unconverted man properly belongs to hell; that is his place; from thence he is, John 8:23. "*Ye are from beneath:*" And thither he is bound; it is the place that justice, and God's word, and the sentence of his unchangeable law assign to him.

4. They are now the objects of that very same *anger* and wrath of God, that is expressed in the torments of hell. And the reason why they do not go down to hell at each moment, is not because God, in whose power they are, is not then very angry with them; as he is with many miserable creatures now tormented in hell, who there feel and bear the fierceness of his wrath. Yea, God is a great deal more angry with great numbers that are now on earth: yea, doubtless, with many that are now in this congregation, who it may be are at ease, than he is with many of those who are now in the flames of hell.

    So that it is not because God is unmindful of their wickedness, and does not resent it, that he does not let loose his hand and cut them off. God is not altogether such an one as themselves, though they may imagine him to be so. The wrath of God burns against them, their damnation does not slumber; the pit is prepared, the fire is made ready, the furnace is now hot, ready to receive them; the flames do now rage and glow. The glittering sword is whet, and held over them, and the pit hath opened its mouth under them.

5. The *devil* stands ready to fall upon them, and seize them as his own, at what moment God shall permit him. They belong to him; he has their souls in his possession, and under his dominion. The

scripture represents them as his goods, Luke 11:12. The devils watch them; they are ever by them at their right hand; they stand waiting for them, like greedy hungry lions that see their prey, and expect to have it, but are for the present kept back. If God should withdraw his hand, by which they are restrained, they would in one moment fly upon their poor souls. The old serpent is gaping for them; hell opens its mouth wide to receive them; and if God should permit it, they would be hastily swallowed up and lost.

6. There are in the souls of wicked men those hellish *principles* reigning, that would presently kindle and flame out into hell fire, if it were not for God's restraints. There is laid in the very nature of carnal men, a foundation for the torments of hell. There are those corrupt principles, in reigning power in them, and in full possession of them, that are seeds of hell fire. These principles are active and powerful, exceeding violent in their nature, and if it were not for the restraining hand of God upon them, they would soon break out, they would flame out after the same manner as the same corruptions, the same enmity does in the hearts of damned souls, and would beget the same torments as they do in them. The souls of the wicked are in scripture compared to the troubled sea, [Isaiah] 57:20. For the present, God restrains their wickedness by his mighty power, as he does the raging waves of the troubled sea, saying, "*Hitherto shalt thou come, but no further;*" but if God should withdraw that restraining power, it would soon carry all before it. Sin is the ruin and misery of the soul; it is destructive in its nature; and if God should leave it without restraint, there would need nothing else to make the soul perfectly miserable.

The corruption of the heart of man is immoderate and boundless in its fury; and while wicked men live here, it is like fire pent up by God's restraints, whereas if it were let loose, it would set on fire the course of nature; and as the heart is now a sink of sin, so if sin was not restrained, it would immediately turn the soul into fiery oven, or a furnace of fire and brimstone.

7.   It is no security to wicked men for one moment, that there are no visible means of death at hand. It is no security to a natural man, that he is now in health, and that he does not see which way he should now immediately go out of the world by any accident, and that there is no visible danger in any respect in his circumstances. The manifold and continual experience of the world in all ages, shows this is no evidence, that a man is not on the very brink of eternity, and that the next step will not be into another world. The unseen, unthought-of ways and means of persons going suddenly out of the world are innumerable and inconceivable. Unconverted men walk over the pit of hell on a rotten covering, and there are innumerable places in this covering so weak that they will not bear their weight, and these places are not seen. The arrows of death fly unseen at noon-day; the sharpest sight cannot discern them. God has so many different unsearchable ways of taking wicked men out of the world and sending them to hell, that there is nothing to make it appear, that God had need to be at the expense of a miracle, or go out of the ordinary course of his providence, to destroy any wicked man, at any moment. All the means that there are of sinners going out of the world, are so in God's hands, and so universally and absolutely subject to his power and determination, that it does not depend at all the less on the mere will

of God, whether sinners shall at any moment go to hell, than if means were never made use of, or at all concerned in the case.

8. Natural men's prudence and care to preserve their own lives, or the care of others to preserve them, do not secure them a moment. To this, divine providence and universal experience do also bear testimony. There is this clear evidence that men's own wisdom is no security to them from death; that if it were otherwise we should see some difference between the wise and politic men of the world, and others, with regard to their liableness to early and unexpected death: but how is it in fact? Eccles. 2:16[:] *"How dieth the wise man? even as the fool."*

9. All wicked men's pains and *contrivance* which they use to escape hell, while they continue to reject Christ, and so remain wicked men, do not secure them from hell one moment. Almost every natural man that hears of hell, flatters himself that he shall escape it; he depends upon himself for his own security; he flatters himself in what he has done, in what he is now doing, or what he intends to do. Every one lays out matters in his own mind how he shall avoid damnation, and flatters himself that he contrives well for himself, and that his schemes will not fail. They hear indeed that there are but few saved, and that the greater part of men that have died heretofore are gone to hell; but each one imagines that he lays out matters better for his own escape than others have done. He does not intend to come to that place of torment; he says within himself, that he intends to take effectual care, and to order matters so for himself as not to fail.

But the foolish children of men miserably delude themselves in their own schemes, and in confidence in their own strength and wisdom; they trust to nothing but a shadow. The greater part of those who heretofore have lived under the same means of grace, and are now dead, are undoubtedly gone to hell; and it was not because they were not as wise as those who are now alive: it was not because they did not lay out matters as well for themselves to secure their own escape. If we could speak with them, and inquire of them, one by one, whether they expected, when alive, and when they used to hear about hell, ever to be the subjects of misery: we doubtless, should hear one and another reply, "No, I never intended to come here: I had laid out matters otherwise in my mind; I thought I should contrive well for myself—I thought my scheme good. I intended to take effectual care; but it came upon me unexpected; I did not look for it at that time, and in that manner; it came as a thief—Death outwitted me: God's wrath was too quick for me. Oh, my cursed foolishness! I was flattering myself, and pleasing myself with vain dreams of what I would do hereafter; and when I was saying, Peace and safety, then sudden destruction came upon me."

10. God has laid himself under no *obligation*, by any promise to keep any natural man out of hell one moment. God certainly has made no promises either of eternal life, or of any deliverance or preservation from eternal death, but what are contained in the covenant of grace, the promises that are given in Christ, in whom all the promises are yea and amen. But surely they have no interest in the promises of the covenant of grace who are not the children of the covenant, who do not believe in any of the promises, and have no interest in the Mediator of the covenant.

So that, whatever some have imagined and pretended about promises made to natural men's earnest seeking and knocking, it is plain and manifest, that whatever pains a natural man takes in religion, whatever prayers he makes, till he believes in Christ, God is under no manner of obligation to keep him a moment from eternal destruction.

So that, thus it is that natural men are held in the hand of God, over the pit of hell; they have deserved the fiery pit, and are already sentenced to it; and God is dreadfully provoked, his anger is as great towards them as to those that are actually suffering the executions of the fierceness of his wrath in hell, and they have done nothing in the least to appease or abate that anger, neither is God in the least bound by any promise to hold them up one moment; the devil is waiting for them, hell is gaping for them, the flames gather and flash about them, and would fain lay hold on them, and swallow them up; the fire pent up in their own hearts is struggling to break out: and they have no interest in any Mediator, there are no means within reach that can be any security to them. In short, they have no refuge, nothing to take hold of; all that preserves them every moment is the mere arbitrary will, and uncovenanted, unobliged forbearance of an incensed God.

APPLICATION

The use of this awful subject may be for awakening unconverted persons in this congregation. This that you have heard is the case of every one of you that are out of Christ.—That world of misery, that take of burning brimstone, is extended abroad under you. There is the dreadful pit of the glowing flames of the wrath of God; there is hell's wide gaping mouth open; and you have nothing to stand upon, nor any thing to take hold of; there is nothing between you and hell but the air; it is only the power and mere pleasure of God that holds you up.

You probably are not sensible of this; you find you are kept out of hell, but do not see the hand of God in it; but look at other things, as the good state of your bodily constitution, your care of your own life, and the means you use for your own preservation. But indeed these things are nothing; if God should withdraw his hand, they would avail no more to keep you from falling, than the thin air to hold up a person that is suspended in it.

Your wickedness makes you as it were heavy as lead, and to tend downwards with great weight and pressure towards hell; and if God should let you go, you would immediately sink and swiftly descend and plunge into the bottomless gulf, and your healthy constitution, and your own care and prudence, and best contrivance, and all your righteousness, would have no more influence to uphold you and keep you out of hell, than a spider's web would have to stop a falling rock. Were it not for the sovereign pleasure of God, the earth would not bear you one moment; for you are a burden to it; the creation groans with you; the creature is made subject to the bondage of your corruption, not willingly; the sun does not willingly shine upon you to give you light to serve sin and Satan; the earth does not willingly yield her increase to satisfy your lusts; nor is it willingly a stage for your wickedness to be acted upon; the air does not willingly serve you for breath to maintain the flame of life in your vitals, while you spend your life in the service of God's enemies. God's creatures are good, and were made for men to serve God with, and do not willingly subserve to any other purpose, and groan when they are abused to purposes so directly contrary to their nature and end. And the world would spew you out, were it not for the sovereign hand of him who hath subjected it in hope. There are the black clouds of God's wrath now hanging directly over your heads, full of the dreadful storm, and big with thunder; and were it not for the restraining hand of God, it would immediately burst forth upon you. The sovereign pleasure of God, for the present, stays his rough wind; otherwise it would come with fury, and your destruction would come like a whirlwind, and you would be like the chaff on the summer threshing floor.

The wrath of God is like great waters that are dammed for the present; they increase more and more, and rise higher and higher, till an outlet is given; and the longer the stream is stopped, the more rapid and mighty is its course, when once it is let loose. It is true, that judgment against your evil works has not been executed hitherto; the floods of God's vengeance have been withheld; but your guilt in the mean time is constantly increasing, and you are every day treasuring up more wrath; the waters are constantly rising, and waxing more and more mighty; and there is nothing but the mere pleasure of God, that holds the waters back, that are unwilling to be stopped, and press hard to go forward. If God should only withdraw his hand from the flood-gate, it would immediately fly open, and the fiery floods of the fierceness and wrath of God, would rush forth with inconceivable fury, and would come upon you with omnipotent power; and if your strength were ten thousand times greater than it is, yea, ten thousand times greater than the strength of the stoutest, sturdiest devil in hell, it would be nothing to withstand or endure it.

The bow of God's wrath is bent, and the arrow made ready on the string, and justice bends the arrow at your heart, and strains the bow, and it is nothing but the mere pleasure of God, and that of an angry God, without any promise or obligation at all, that keeps the arrow one moment from being made drunk with your blood. Thus all you that never passed under a great change of heart, by the mighty power of the Spirit of God upon your souls; all you that were never born again, and made new creatures, and raised from being dead in sin, to a state of new, and before altogether unexperienced light and life, are in the hands of an angry God. However you may have reformed your life in many things, and may have had religious affections, and may keep up a form of religion in your families and closets, and in the house of God, it is nothing but his mere pleasure that keeps you from being this moment swallowed up in everlasting destruction. However unconvinced you may now be of the truth of what you hear, by and by you will be fully convinced of it. Those that are gone from being in the like circumstances with you, see that it was so with them; for destruction came suddenly upon most of them; when they expected nothing of it, and while they were saying, Peace and safety: now they see, that those things on which they depended for peace and safety, were nothing but thin air and empty shadows.

The God that holds you over the pit of hell, much as one holds a spider, or some loathsome insect over the fire, abhors you, and is dreadfully provoked: his wrath towards you burns like fire; he looks upon you as worthy of nothing else, but to be cast into the fire; he is of purer eyes than to bear to have you in his sight; you are ten thousand times more abominable in his eyes, than the most hateful venomous serpent is in ours. You have offended him infinitely more than ever a stubborn rebel did his prince; and yet it is nothing but his hand that holds you from falling into the fire every moment. It is to be ascribed to nothing else, that you did not go to hell the last night; that you was suffered to awake again in this world, after you closed your eyes to sleep. And there is no other reason to be given, why you have not dropped into hell since you arose in the morning, but that God's hand has held you up. There is no other reason to be given why you have not gone to hell, since you have sat here in the house of God, provoking his pure eyes by your sinful wicked manner of attending his solemn worship. Yea, there is nothing else that is to be given as a reason why you do not this very moment drop down into hell.

O sinner! Consider the fearful danger you are in: it is a great furnace of wrath, a wide and bottomless pit, full of the fire of wrath, that you are held over in the hand of that God, whose wrath is provoked and incensed as much against you, as against many of the damned in hell. You hang by a slender thread, with the flames of divine wrath flashing about it, and ready every moment to singe it, and burn it asunder; and you have no interest in any Mediator, and nothing to lay hold of to save yourself, nothing to keep off the flames of wrath, nothing of your own, nothing that you ever have done, nothing that you can do, to induce God to spare you one moment.—And consider here more particularly,

1. *Whose* wrath it is: it is the wrath of the infinite God. If it were only the wrath of man, though it were of the most potent prince, it would be comparatively little to be regarded. The wrath of kings is very much dreaded, especially of absolute monarchs, who have the possessions and lives of their subjects wholly in their power, to be disposed of at their mere will. [Proverbs] 20:2. "*The fear of a king is as the roaring of a lion: Whoso provoketh him to anger, sinneth against his own soul.*" The subject that very much enrages an arbitrary prince, is liable to suffer the most extreme torments that human art can invent, or human power can inflict. But the greatest earthly potentates in their greatest majesty and strength, and when clothed in their greatest terrors, are but feeble, despicable worms of the dust, in comparison of the great and almighty Creator and King of heaven and earth. It is but little that they can do, when most enraged, and when they have exerted the utmost of their fury. All the kings of the earth, before God, are as grasshoppers; they are nothing, and less than nothing: both their love and their hatred is to be despised. The wrath of the great King of kings, is as much more terrible than theirs, as his majesty is greater. Luke 12:4–5. "*And I say unto you, my friends, Be not afraid of them that kill the body, and after that, have no more that they can do. But I will forewarn you whom you shall fear: fear him, which after he hath killed, hath power to cast into hell: yea, I say unto you, Fear him.*"

2. It is the *fierceness* of his wrath that you are exposed to. We often read of the fury of God; as in [Isaiah] 59:18.

"*According to their deeds, accordingly he will repay fury to his adversaries.*" So [Isaiah] 66:15. "*For behold, the Lord will come with fire, and with his chariots like a whirlwind, to render his anger with fury, and his rebuke with flames of fire.*" And in many other places. So, [Revelations] 19:15, we read of "*the wine press of the fierceness and wrath of Almighty God.*" The words are exceeding terrible. If it had only been said, "*the wrath of God,*" the words would have implied that which is infinitely dreadful: but it is "*the fierceness and wrath of God.*" The fury of God! the fierceness of Jehovah! Oh, how dreadful that must be! Who can utter or conceive what such expressions carry in them! But it is also "*the fierceness and wrath of almighty God.*" As though there would be a very great manifestation of his almighty power in what the fierceness of his wrath should inflict, as though omnipotence should be as it were enraged, and exerted, as men are wont to exert their strength in the fierceness of their wrath. Oh! then, what will be the consequence! What will become of the poor worms that shall suffer it! Whose hands can be strong? And whose heart can endure? To what a dreadful, inexpressible, inconceivable depth of misery must the poor creature be sunk who shall be the subject of this!

Consider this, you that are here present, that yet remain in an unregenerate state. That God will execute the fierceness of his anger, implies, that he will inflict wrath without any pity. When God beholds the ineffable extremity of your case, and sees your torment to be so vastly disproportioned to your strength, and sees how your poor soul is crushed, and sinks down, as it were, into an infinite gloom; he will have no compassion upon you, he will not forbear the executions of his wrath, or in the least lighten his hand; there shall be no moderation or mercy, nor will God then at all stay his rough wind; he will have no regard to your welfare, nor be at all careful lest you should suffer too much in any other sense, than only that you shall *not suffer beyond what strict justice requires.* Nothing shall be withheld, because it is so hard for you to bear. [Ezekiel] 8:18. *"Therefore will I also deal in fury: mine eye shall not spare, neither will I have pity; and though they cry in mine ears with a loud voice, yet I will not hear them."* Now God stands ready to pity you; this is a day of mercy; you may cry now with some encouragement of obtaining mercy. But when once the day of mercy is past, your most lamentable and dolorous cries and shrieks will be in vain; you will be wholly lost and thrown away of God, as to any regard to your welfare. God will have no other use to put you to, but to suffer misery; you shall be continued in being to no other end; for you will be a vessel of wrath fitted to destruction; and there will be no other use of this vessel, but to be filled full of wrath. God will be so far from pitying you when you cry to him, that it is said he will only *"laugh and mock,"* [Proverbs 1:25, 26, &c.]

How awful are those words, [Isaiah] 63:3, which are the words of the great God. *"I will tread them in mine anger, and will trample them in my fury, and their blood shall be sprinkled upon my garments, and I will stain all my raiment."* It is perhaps impossible to conceive of words that carry in them greater manifestations of these three things, viz. contempt, and hatred, and fierceness of indignation. If you cry to God to pity you, he will be so far from pitying you in your doleful case, or showing you the least regard or favour, that instead of that, he will only tread you under foot. And though he will know that you cannot bear the weight of omnipotence treading upon you, yet he will not regard that, but he will crush you under his feet without mercy; he will crush out your blood, and make it fly, and it shall be sprinkled on his garments, so as to stain all his raiment. He will not only hate you, but he will have you in the utmost contempt: no place shall be thought fit for you, but under his feet to be trodden down as the mire of the streets.

3. The *misery* you are exposed to is that which God will inflict to that end, that he might show what that wrath of Jehovah is. God hath had it on his heart to show to angels and men, both how excellent his love is, and also how terrible his wrath is. Sometimes earthly kings have a mind to show how terrible their wrath is, by the extreme punishments they would execute on those that would provoke them. Nebuchadnezzar, that mighty and haughty monarch of the Chaldean empire, was willing to show his wrath when enraged with Shadrach, Meshach, and Abednego; and accordingly gave orders that the burning fiery furnace should be heated seven times hotter than it was before; doubtless, it was raised to the utmost degree of fierceness that human art could raise it. But the great God is also willing to show his wrath, and magnify his awful majesty and mighty power in the extreme sufferings of his enemies. [Romans] 9:22. "*What if God, willing to show his wrath, and to make his power known, endured with much long-suffering the vessels of wrath fitted to destruction?*" And seeing this is his design, and what he has determined, even to show how terrible the unrestrained wrath, the fury and fierceness of Jehovah is, he will do it to effect. There will be something accomplished and brought to pass that will be dreadful with a witness. When the great and angry God hath risen up and executed his awful vengeance on the poor

sinner, and the wretch is actually suffering the infinite weight and power of his indignation, then will God call upon the whole universe to behold that awful majesty and mighty power that is to be seen in it. [Isaiah] 33:12–14. *"And the people shall be as the burnings of lime, as thorns cut up shall they be burnt in the fire. Hear ye that are far off, what I have done; and ye that are near, acknowledge my might. The sinners in Zion are afraid; fearfulness hath surprised the hypocrites,"* &c.

Thus it will be with you that are in an unconverted state, if you continue in it; the infinite might, and majesty, and terribleness of the omnipotent God shall be magnified upon you, in the ineffable strength of your torments. You shall be tormented in the presence of the holy angels, and in the presence of the Lamb; and when you shall be in this state of suffering, the glorious inhabitants of heaven shall go forth and look on the awful spectacle, that they may see what the wrath and fierceness of the Almighty is; and when they have seen it, they will fall down and adore that great power and majesty. [Isaiah] 66:23–24. *"And it shall come to pass, that from one new moon to another, and from one sabbath to another, shall all flesh come to worship before me, saith the Lord. And they shall go forth and look upon the carcasses of the men that have transgressed against me; for their worm shall not die, neither shall their fire be quenched, and they shall be an abhorring unto all flesh."*

4. It is *everlasting* wrath. It would be dreadful to suffer this fierceness and wrath of Almighty God one moment; but you must suffer it to all eternity. There will be no end to this exquisite horrible misery. When you look forward, you shall see a long for ever, a boundless duration before you, which will swallow

up your thoughts, and amaze your soul; and you will absolutely despair of ever having any deliverance, any end, any mitigation, any rest at all. You will know certainly that you must wear out long ages, millions of millions of ages, in wrestling and conflicting with this almighty merciless vengeance; and then when you have so done, when so many ages have actually been spent by you in this manner, you will know that all is but a point to what remains. So that your punishment will indeed be infinite. Oh, who can express what the state of a soul in such circumstances is! All that we can possibly say about it, gives but a very feeble, faint representation of it; it is inexpressible and inconceivable: For "*who knows the power of God's anger?*"

How dreadful is the state of those that are daily and hourly in the danger of this great wrath and infinite misery! But this is the dismal case of every soul in this congregation that has not been born again, however moral and strict, sober and religious, they may otherwise be. Oh that you would consider it, whether you be young or old! There is reason to think, that there are many in this congregation now hearing this discourse, that will actually be the subjects of this very misery to all eternity. We know not who they are, or in what seats they sit, or what thoughts they now have. It may be they are now at ease, and hear all these things without much disturbance, and are now flattering themselves that they are not the persons, promising themselves that they shall escape. If we knew that there was one person, and but one, in the whole congregation, that was to be the subject of this misery, what an awful thing would it be to think of! If we knew who it was, what an awful sight would it be to see such a person! How might all the rest of the congregation lift up a lamentable and bitter cry over him! But, alas! instead of one, how many is it likely will remember this discourse in hell? And it would be a wonder, if some that are now present should not be in hell in a very short time, even before this year is out. And it would be no wonder if some persons, that now sit here, in some seats of this meeting-house, in health, quiet and secure, should be there before tomorrow morning. Those of you that finally continue in a natural condition, that shall keep out of hell longest will be there in a little time! your damnation does not slumber; it will come swiftly, and, in all probability, very suddenly upon many of you. You have reason to wonder that you are not already in hell. It is doubtless the case of some whom you have seen and known, that never deserved hell more than you, and that heretofore appeared as likely to have been now alive as you. Their case is past all hope; they are crying in extreme misery and perfect despair; but here you are in the land of the living and in the house of God, and have an opportunity to obtain salvation. What would not those poor damned hopeless souls give for one day's opportunity such as you now enjoy!

And now you have an extraordinary opportunity, a day wherein Christ has thrown the door of mercy wide open, and stands in calling and crying with a loud voice to poor sinners; a day wherein many are flocking to him, and pressing into the kingdom of God. Many are daily coming from the east, west, north and south; many that were very lately in the same miserable condition that you are in, are now in a happy state, with their hearts filled with love to him who has loved them, and washed them from their sins in his own blood, and rejoicing in hope of the glory of God. How awful is it to be left behind at such a day! To see so many others feasting, while you are pining and perishing! To see so many rejoicing and singing for joy of heart, while you have cause to mourn for sorrow of heart, and howl for vexation of spirit! How can you rest one moment in such a condition? Are not your souls as precious as the souls of the people at Suffield, where they are flocking from day to day to Christ?

Are there not many here who have lived long in the world, and are not to this day born again? and so are aliens from the commonwealth of Israel, and have done nothing ever since they have lived, but treasure up wrath against the day of wrath? Oh, sirs, your case, in an especial manner, is extremely dangerous. Your guilt and hardness of heart is extremely great. Do you not see how generality persons of your years are passed over and left, in the present remarkable and wonderful dispensation of God's mercy? You had need to consider yourselves, and awake thoroughly out of sleep. You cannot bear the fierceness and wrath of the infinite God.—And you, young men, and young women, will you neglect this precious season which you now enjoy, when so many others of your age are renouncing all youthful vanities, and flocking to Christ? You especially have now an extraordinary opportunity; but if you neglect it, it will soon be with you as with those persons who spent all the precious days of youth in sin, and are now come to such a dreadful pass in blindness and hardness.—And you, children, who are unconverted, do not you know that you are going down to hell, to bear the dreadful wrath of that God, who is now angry with you every day and every night? Will you be content to be the children of the devil, when so many other children in the land are converted, and are become the holy and happy children of the King of kings?

And let every one that is yet out of Christ, and hanging over the pit of hell, whether they be old men and women, or middle aged, or young people, or little children, now hearken to the loud calls of God's word and providence. This acceptable year of the Lord, a day of such great favour to some, will doubtless be a day of as remarkable vengeance to others. Men's hearts harden, and their guilt increases apace at such a day as this, if they neglect their souls; and never was there so great danger of such persons being given up to hardness of heart and blindness of mind. God seems now to be hastily gathering in his elect in all parts of the land; and probably the greater part of adult persons that ever shall be saved, will be brought in now in a little time, and that it will be as it was on the great out-pouring of the Spirit upon the Jews in the apostles' days; the election will obtain, and the rest will be blinded. If this should be the case with you, you will eternally curse this day, and will curse the day that ever you was born, to see such a season of the pouring out of God's Spirit, and will wish that you had died and gone to hell before you had seen it. Now undoubtedly it is, as it was in the days of John the Baptist, the axe is in an extraordinary manner laid at the root of the trees, that every tree which brings not forth good fruit, may be hewn down and cast into the fire.

Therefore, let every one that is out of Christ, now awake and fly from the wrath to come. The wrath of Almighty God is now undoubtedly hanging over a great part of this congregation. Let every one fly out of Sodom: "Haste and escape for your lives, look not behind you, escape to the mountain, lest you be consumed."

AN EXCERPT FROM EDWARDS'S SERMON
"WICKED MEN USEFUL IN THEIR DESTRUCTION ONLY"

"Son of man, What is the vine tree more than any tree?
Or than a branch which is among the trees of the forest?
Shall wood be taken thereof to do any work?
Or will men take a pin of it to hang any vessel thereon?
Behold, it is cast into the fire for fuel; The fire
devoureth both the ends of it, and the midst of it
is burnt: Is it meet for any work?"

Ezekiel 15:2–4

The visible church of God is here compared to the vine tree, as is evident by God's own explanation of the allegory, in verses 6, 7, and 8. "Therefore thus saith the Lord God, As the vine tree among the trees of the forest, which I have given to the fire for fuel, so will I give the inhabitants of Jerusalem," &c. And it may be understood of mankind in general. We find man often in scripture compared to a vine. So in chapter 32 of Deuteronomy, "Their vine is the vine of Sodom, and of the fields of Gomorrah. Their grapes are grapes of gall." And Psalm lxxx. 8. "Thou hast brought a vine out of Egypt;" verse 14. "Look down from heaven, behold, and visit this vine." And Canticles ii. 15. "The foxes that spoil the vines; for our vines have tender grapes." Isaiah v. at the beginning, "My beloved hath a vineyard, and he planted it with the choicest vine." Jeremiah ii. 2l. "I had planted thee a noble vine." Hosea x. 1. "Israel is an empty vine." So in chapter 15 of John, visible Christians are compared to the branches of a vine.

Man is very fitly represented by the vine. The weakness and dependence of the vine on other things which support it, well represents to us what a poor, feeble, dependent creature man is, and how, if left to himself, he must fall into mischief, and cannot help himself. The visible people of God are fitly compared to a vine, because of the care and cultivation of the husbandman, or vine dresser. The business of husbandmen in the land of Israel was very much in their vineyards, about vines; and the care they exercised to fence them, to defend them, to prune them, to prop them up, and to cultivate them, well represented that merciful care which God exercises towards his visible people; and this latter is often in scripture expressly compared to the former.

In the words now read is represented,

1. How wholly useless and unprofitable, even beyond other trees, a vine is, in case of unfruitfulness: "What is a vine tree more than any tree, or than a branch which is among the trees of the forest?" i.e. if it do not bear fruit. Men make much more of a vine than of other trees; they take great care of it, to wall it in, to dig about it, to prune it, and the like. It is much more highly esteemed than any one of the trees of the forest; they are despised in comparison with it. And if it bear fruit, it is indeed much preferable to other trees; for the fruit of it yields a noble liquor; as it is said in Jotham's parable, Judges ix. 13. "And the vine said unto them, Should I leave my wine, which cheereth God and man?" But if it bear no fruit, it is more unprofitable than the trees of the forest; for the wood of them is good for timber; but the wood of the vine is fit for no work; as in the text, "Shall wood be taken thereof to do any work? Or will men take a pin of it to hang any vessel thereon?"

2. The only thing for which a vine is useful, in case of barrenness, viz. for fuel: "Behold, it is cast into the fire for fuel." It is wholly consumed; no part of it is worth a saving, to make any instrument of it, for any work.

DOCTRINE

If men bring forth no fruit to God, they are wholly useless, unless in their destruction.

For the proof of this doctrine, I shall show,

1. That it is very evident, that there can be but two ways in which man can be useful, viz. either in acting, or in being acted upon, and disposed of.

2. That man can no otherwise be useful actively than by bringing forth fruit to God.

3. That if he bring not forth fruit to God, there is no other way in which he can be passively useful, but in being destroyed.

4. In that way he may be useful without bearing fruit.

I. There are but two ways in which man can be useful, viz. either in acting or being acted upon. If man be an useful sort of creature, he must be so either actively or passively: There is no medium. If he be useful to any purpose, he must be so either in acting himself, or else in being disposed of by some other; either in doing something himself to that purpose, or else in having something done upon him by some other to that purpose. What can be more plain, than that if man do nothing himself, and nothing be done with him or upon him by any other, he cannot be any way at all useful? If man do nothing himself to promote the end of his existence, and no other being do any thing with him to promote this end, then nothing will be done to promote this end; and so man must be wholly useless. So that there are but two ways in which man can be useful to any purpose, viz. either actively or passively, either in doing something himself, or in being the subject of something done to him.

II.   Man cannot be useful actively, any otherwise than in bringing forth fruit to God, than in serving God, and living to his glory. This is the only way wherein he can be useful in doing; and that for this reason, that the glory of God is the very thing for which man was made, and to which all other ends are subordinate. Man is not an independent being, but he derives his being from another; and therefore hath his end assigned him by that other: And he that gave him his being, made him for the end now mentioned. This was the very design and aim of the Author of man, this was the work for which he made him, viz. to serve and glorify his Maker.

Other creatures are made for inferior purposes. Inferior creatures were made for inferior purposes. But it is to be observed, that man is the creature that is highest, and nearest to God, of any in this lower world; and therefore his business is with God, although other creatures are made for lower ends. There my be observed a kind of gradation, or gradual ascent, in the order of the different kinds of creatures, from the meanest clod of earth to man, who hath a rational and immortal soul. A plant, an herb, or tree, is superior in nature to a stone or clod, because it hath a vegetable life. The brute creatures are a degree higher still; for they have sensitive life. But man, having a rational soul, is the highest of this lower creation, and is next to God; therefore his business is with God.

Things without life, as earth, water, &c. are subservient to things above them, as the grass, herbs and trees. These vegetables are subservient to that order of creatures which is next above them, the brute creation; they are for food to them. Brute creatures, again, are made for the use and service of the order above them; they are made for the service of mankind. But man being the highest of this lower creation, the next step from him is to God. He therefore is made for the service and glory of God. This is the whole work and business of man; it is his highest end, to which all other ends are subordinate.

If it had not been for this end, there never would have been any such sort of creature as man; there would have been no occasion for it. Other inferior ends may be answered as well, without any such creature as man. There would have been no sort of occasion for making so noble a creature, and endowing him with such faculties, only to enjoy earthly good, to eat, and to drink, and to enjoy sensual things. Brute creatures, without reason, are capable of these things, as well as man; Yea, if no higher end be aimed at than to enjoy sensitive good, reason is rather an hinderance than an help. It doth but render man the more capable of afflicting himself with care, and fears of death, and other future evils, and of vexing himself with many anxieties, from which brute creatures are wholly free, and therefore can gratify their senses with less molestation. Besides, reason doth but make men more capable of molesting and impeding one another in the gratification of their senses. If man have no other end to seek but to gratify his senses, reason is nothing but an impediment.

Therefore if man be not made to serve and glorify his Creator, it is wholly to no purpose that such a creature is made. Doubtless then the all wise God, who doth all things in infinite wisdom, hath made man for this end. And this is agreeable to what he hath taught us in many places in the scriptures. This is the great end for which man was made, and for which he was made such a creature as he is, having a body and soul, bodily senses, and rational powers. For this is he placed in such circumstances as he is, and the earth is given him for a possession. For this he hath dominion given him over the rest of the creatures of this world. For this the sun shines on him, and the moon and stars are for signs and seasons to him, and the rain falls on him, and the earth yields him her increase.

THE DAY OF DOOM

Michael Wigglesworth

Still was the night, Serene & Bright,
when all Men sleeping lay;
Calm was the season, & carnal reason
thought so 'twould last for ay.
Soul, take thine ease, let sorrow cease,
much good thou hast in store:
This was their Song, their Cups among,
the Evening before.

Wallowing in all kind of sin,
vile wretches lay secure:
The best of men had scarcely then
their Lamps kept in good ure.
Virgins unwise, who through disguise
amongst the best were number'd,
Had closed their eyes; yea, and the wise
through sloth and frailty slumber'd.

For at midnight brake forth a Light,
which turn'd the night to day,
And speedily a hideous cry
did all the world dismay.
Sinners awake, their hearts do ake,
trembling their loynes surprizeth;
Amaz'd with fear, by what they hear,
each one of them ariseth.

They rush from Beds with giddy heads,
and to their windows run,
Viewing this light, which shines more bright
than doth the Noon-day Sun.
Straightway appears (they see 't with tears)

the Son of God most dread;
Who with his Train comes on amain
to Judge both Quick and Dead.

Before his face the Heav'ns gave place,
and Skies are rent asunder,
With mighty voice, and hideous noise,
more terrible than Thunder.
His brightness damps heav'ns glorious lamps
and makes them hang their heads,
As if afraid and quite dismay'd,
they quit their wonted steads.

No heart so bold, but now grows cold
and almost dead with fear:
No eye so dry, but now can cry,
and pour out many a tear.
Earth's Potentates and pow'rful States,
Captains and Men of Might
Are quite abasht, their courage dasht
at this most dreadful sight.

Mean men lament, great men do rent
their Robes, and tear their hair:
They do not spare their flesh to tear
through horrible despair.
All Kindreds wail: all hearts do fail:
horror the world doth fill
With weeping eyes, and loud out-cries,
yet knows not how to kill.

Some hide themselves in Caves and Delves,
in places under ground:
Some rashly leap into the Deep,
to scape by being drown'd:
Some to the Rocks (O senseless blocks!)

and woody Mountains run,
That there they might this fearful sight,
and dreaded Presence shun.

In vain do they to Mountains say,
fall on us and us hide
From Judges ire, more hot than fire,
for who may it abide?
No hiding place can from his Face
sinners at all conceal,
Whose flaming Eye hid things doth 'spy
and darkest things reveal.

The Judge draws nigh, exalted high,
upon a lofty Throne,
Amidst a throng of Angels strong,
lo, Israel's Holy One!
The excellence of whose presence
and awful Majesty,
Amazeth Nature, and every Creature,
doth more than terrify.

The Mountains smoak, the Hills are shook,
the Earth is rent and torn,
As if she should be clear dissolv'd,
or from the Center born.
The Sea doth roar, forsakes the shore,
and shrinks away for fear;
The wild beasts flee into the Sea,
so soon as he draws near.

Before his Throne a Trump is blown,
Proclaiming the day of Doom:
Forthwith he cries, Ye dead arise,
and unto Judgment come.
No sooner said, but 'tis obey'd;

Sepulchres opened are:
Dead bodies all rise at his call,
and 's mighty power declare.

His winged Hosts flie through all Coasts,
together gathering
Both good and bad, both quick and dead,
and all to Judgment bring.
Out of their holes those creeping Moles,
that hid themselves for fear,
By force they take, and quickly make
before the Judge appear.

Thus every one before the Throne
of Christ the Judge is brought,
Both righteous and impious
that good or ill hath wrought.
A separation, and diff'ring station
by Christ appointed is
(To sinners sad)'twixt good and bad,
'twixt Heirs of woe and bliss.

CHRONOLOGY & TIMELINE

1694   The Reverend Timothy Edwards marries Esther Stoddard.

1703   Jonathan Edwards is born in East Windsor, Connecticut.

1716   Jonathan Edwards enters the Wethersfield branch of
the Collegiate School.

1718   The Collegiate School is renamed Yale College.

1720   Jonathan Edwards graduates first in his class from Yale.

1721   Edwards has the beginning of his religious experience.

1722   Edwards goes to New York City as a Presbyterian pastor.

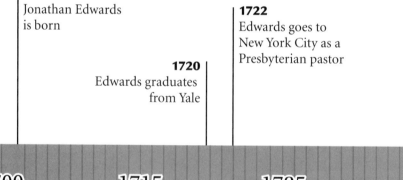

1703
Jonathan Edwards
is born

1722
Edwards goes to
New York City as a
Presbyterian pastor

1720
Edwards graduates
from Yale

1700   1715   1725

1723
Edwards gives his oration
at Yale's Commencement

1727
Edwards is ordained in Northampton
and marries Sarah Pierpont

1723   Edwards gives a public oration at the Yale Commencement. He later returns to Yale and meets Sarah Pierpont.

1724   Edwards serves as pastor of Bolton, Connecticut, and later returns to Yale as a college tutor.

1726   Edwards is called to Northampton, Massachusetts.

1727   Edwards is ordained in Northampton. He marries Sarah Pierpont.

1729   The Reverend Solomon Stoddard dies, and Edwards becomes sole pastor.

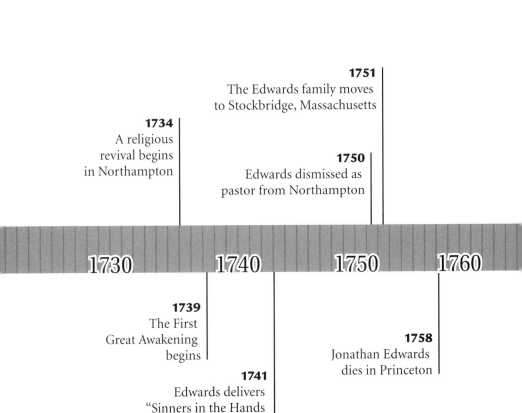

1751
The Edwards family moves
to Stockbridge, Massachusetts

1734
A religious
revival begins
in Northampton

1750
Edwards dismissed as
pastor from Northampton

1730   1740   1750   1760

1739
The First
Great Awakening
begins

1758
Jonathan Edwards
dies in Princeton

1741
Edwards delivers
"Sinners in the Hands
of an Angry God"

CHRONOLOGY

1731 Edwards delivers the commencement sermon at Harvard.

1734 A religious revival begins in Northampton.

1735 Edwards's uncle, Joseph Hawley, commits suicide.

1736 Edwards writes the *Narrative of Surprising Conversions in Northampton and Vicinity.*

1739 The First Great Awakening begins.

1740 Edwards entertains George Whitefield in Northampton.

1741 Edwards delivers his greatest sermon, "Sinners in the Hands of an Angry God."

1744 King George's War, between England and France, begins.

1747 David Brainerd dies at the Edwards home in Northampton.

1748 Jerusha Edwards dies at the family home.

1748–1749 Controversy erupts over open admission to the Lord's Supper.

1750 Edwards is dismissed as pastor from Northampton, Massachussets.

1751 The Edwards family moves to Stockbridge, Massachusetts.

1752 Esther Edwards marries the Reverend Aaron Burr.

1754 The French and Indian War begins. The Reverend Aaron Burr dies in New Jersey and Edwards receives a call to be president of the College of New Jersey.

1758 The Reverend Timothy Edwards dies in East Windsor. Jonathan Edwards dies in Princeton. Esther Edwards Burr dies in Princeton. Sarah Edwards dies in Philadelphia.

1771 Esther Stoddard Edwards dies in East Windsor, Connecticut, at the age of 98.

NOTES

CHAPTER 1: A Man of God

1. S. E. Dwight, *The Life of President Edwards.* New York: G & C & H Carvill, 1830, p. 72.

2. George M. Marsden, *Jonathan Edwards: A Life.* New Haven, Conn.: Yale University Press, 2003, p. 83.

3. Dwight, *President Edwards*, p. 92.

4. Kenneth P. Minkema, ed., *The Works of Jonathan Edwards*, vol. 14. New Haven, Conn.: Yale University Press, 1997, p. 60.

5. Ibid.

6. Ibid.

7. Ibid., p. 61.

8. Ibid., p. 64.

9. Clarence H. Faust and Thomas H. Johnson, *Jonathan Edwards: Representative Selections, with Introduction, Bibliography, and Notes.* New York: American Book Company, 1935, p. 46.

10. Arthur Cushman McGiffert, Jr., *Jonathan Edwards.* New York: Harper & Brothers, 1932, pp. 38–39.

CHAPTER 2: A Minister and His Family

11. Ola Elizabeth Winslow, *Jonathan Edwards.* New York: Macmillan, 1940, p. 49.

12. Ibid., pp. 49–50.

13. Ibid., p. 50.

CHAPTER 3: Yale College

14. Edwin Oviatt, *The Beginnings of Yale, 1701–1726.* New Haven, Conn.: Yale University Press., 1916, pp. 348–353.

15. Winslow, *Jonathan Edwards*, p. 72.

16. Jonathan Edwards., "Conversion of President Edwards," in *A Narrative of Many Surprising Conversions in Northampton and Vicinity.* Worcester, Mass.: Moses W. Grout, 1832, p. 367.

17. Ibid., p. 368.

18. Faust and Johnson, *Jonathan Edwards*, p. 64.

19. Ibid.

20. Ibid, pp. 64–65.

21. Edwards, "Conversion of President Edwards," p. 374.

CHAPTER 4: Northampton

22. Jonathan Edwards, *A Narrative of Many Surprising Conversions in Northampton and Vicinity.* Worcester, Mass.: Moses W. Grout, 1832, p. 1.

23. Ibid.

24. Ibid., pp. 6–7.

25. Ibid., p. 7.

26. Ibid., p. 9.

27. Ibid., p. 10.

28. Faust and Johnson, *Jonathan Edwards*, p. 77.

29. Ibid.

30. Faust and Johnson, *Jonathan Edwards*, p. 79.

31. Ibid., p. 83.

32. Ibid.

CHAPTER 5: The Great Awakening

33. Dwight, *President Edwards*, p. 139.

34. Ibid., p. 140.

35. Joseph Belcher, D.D., *George Whitefield: A Biography, with special reference to his labors in America.* New York: American Tract Society, 1857, pp. 179–180.

36. Ibid., p. 184.

37. Michael J. Crawford, "The Spiritual Travels of Nathan Cole," *William and Mary Quarterly.* January 1976, pp. 92–93.

38. Faust and Johnson, *Jonathan Edwards*, p. 155.

39. Ibid., p. 156.

40. Ibid., pp. 157–158.

41. Ibid., p. 161.

42. Ibid.

43. Ibid., p. 162.

44. Ibid., pp. 171–172.

CHAPTER 6: The Edwards Home

45. Elisabeth D. Dodds, *Marriage to a Difficult Man: The "Uncommon Union" of Jonathan and Sarah Edwards.* Philadelphia: Westminster Press, 1971, p. 36.

46. Dwight, *The Life of President Edwards*, p. 172.

47. Dodds, *Marriage*, p. 100.

48. Ibid.

49. Minkema, ed., *The Life of David Brainerd*, *The Works of Jonathan Edwards*, vol , pp. 313–314.

CHAPTER 7: A Prophet Without Honor

50. Dwight, *The Life of President Edwards*, pp. 630–631.

51. Ibid., p. 646.

CHAPTER 8: Mission to the Indians

52. Marsden, *Jonathan Edwards*, p. 407.

53. Ibid., p. 415.

CHAPTER 9: A Ray of Light and a Dark Cloud

54. Dwight, *The Life of President Edwards*, p. 568.

55. Ibid.

56. Marsden, *Jonathan Edwards*, p. 494.

57. Carol F. Karlsen and Laurie Crumpacker, eds., *The Journal of Esther Edwards Burr, 1754–1757*. New Haven, Conn.: Yale University Press, 1984, p. 301.

CHAPTER 10: Jonathan Edwards's Legacy

58. Perry Miller, *Jonathan Edwards*. New York: William Sloane Associates, 1949, pp. xxi–xxii.

59. Patricia J. Tracy, *Jonathan Edwards, Pastor*. New York: Hill & Wang, 1980, p. 92.

60. Marsden, *Jonathan Edwards*, pp. 504–505.

GLOSSARY

Anglican—A member of the Anglican Church, also known as the Church of England.

Baptist—One who belives in the concept of adult, as opposed to infant, baptism.

Calvinist—A follower of the teachings of John Calvin, a sixteenth-century Frenchman.

Catholic—Also Roman Catholic. Those who followed the teachings of the church based in the Vatican and presided over by the Pope.

Communion—The Roman Catholic rite of consuming the consecrated bread to reenact the last supper of Jesus Christ.

Lord's Supper—The Protestant rite which parallels the Catholic Communion.

Lutheran—A follower of the teachings of the sixteenth-century monk Martin Luther.

Papist—The derogatory term that Protestants used to describe Roman Catholics, derived from the word for the leader of the Roman Catholic Church, the Pope.

Predestination—The belief that God decides before a person is even born whether or not that person will be saved.

Protestant—An umbrella term used to describe the different churches that resulted from the Protestant Reformation.

Puritan—One who "purifies." The Puritans wanted to purify the Church of England (Anglican Church) which had been created in the time of King Henry VIII.

Revival—Usually means a "revival of religion." Was frequently used in the New England churches to intensify the faith of the parishioners.

Salvation—A term that is used with different definitions by different faiths. To the New England Puritans, salvation meant a personal experience of Jesus Christ.

Belcher, Joseph, D.D. *George Whitefield: A Biography, with special reference to his labors in America.* New York: American Tract Society, 1857.

Carnes, Mark, and John Garraty. *American National Biography,* vol. 10. New York: Oxford University Press, 1999.

Crawford, Michael J. "The Spiritual Travels of Nathan Cole." *William and Mary Quarterly.* January 1976. pp. 92–93.

Dodds, Elisabeth D. *Marriage to a Difficult Man: The "Uncommon Union" of Jonathan and Sarah Edwards.* Philadelphia: Westminster Press, 1971.

Dwight, Sereno. *The Life of President Edwards.* New York: G & C & H Carvill, 1830.

Edwards, Jonathan. *A Narrative of Many Surprising Conversions in Northampton and Vicinity.* Worcester, Mass.: Moses W. Grout, 1832.

Faust, Clarence H., and Thomas H. Johnson, eds. *Jonathan Edwards: Representative Selections, with Introduction, Bibliography, and Notes.* New York: The American Book Company, 1935.

Frazier, Patrick. *The Mohicans of Stockbridge.* Lincoln, Neb.: University of Nebraska Press, 1992.

Karlsen, Carol F., and Laurie Crumpacker, eds. *The Journal of Esther Edwards Burr, 1754–1757.* New Haven, Conn.: Yale Universtiy Press, 1984.

MacLean, John. *History of the College of New Jersey, from its origin in 1746 to the commencement of 1854.* Philadelphia: J.B. Lippincott, 1877.

McGiffert, Arthur Cushman, Jr. *Jonathan Edwards.* New York: Harper & Brothers, 1932.

Marsden, George M. *Jonathan Edwards: A Life.* New Haven, Conn.: Yale University Press, 2003.

Miller, Perry. *Jonathan Edwards.* New York: William Sloane Associates, 1949.

BIBLIOGRAPHY

Minkema, Kenneth P. "Hannah and Her Sisters: Sisterhood, Courtship, and Marriage in the Edwards Family in the Early Eighteenth Century." *New England Historical and Genealogical Register,* 1992.

———, ed. *The Works of Jonathan Edwards.* New Haven, Conn.: Yale University Press, 1997.

Oviatt, Edwin. *The Beginnings of Yale (1701–1726).* New Haven, Conn.: Yale University Press, 1916.

Pollock, John. *George Whitefield and the Great Awakening.* New York: Doubleday, 1972.

Porterfield, Amanda. *Feminine Spirituality in America: From Sarah Edwards to Martha Graham.* Philadelphia: Temple University Press, 1980.

Shea, Daniel B. Jr., *Spiritual Autobiography in Early America.* Princeton, N.J.: Princeton University Press, 1968.

Tracy, Patricia J. *Jonathan Edwards, Pastor: Religion and Society in Eighteenth-Century Northampton.* New York: Hill and Wang, 1980.

Warch, Richard. *School of the Prophets: Yale College, 1701–1740.* New Haven, Conn.: Yale University Press, 1973.

Winslow, Ola Elizabeth. *Jonathan Edwards, 1703–1758: A Biography.* New York: The Macmillan Company, 1940.

INDEX

INDEX

INDEX

PICTURE CREDITS

ABOUT THE CONTRIBUTORS

SAMUEL WILLARD CROMPTON lives near Northampton, Massachusetts, which was Jonathan Edwards's parish for many years. Crompton teaches history at Holyoke Community College. He is the author or editor of many books, such as *100 Spiritual Leaders Who Shaped World History*, *Martin Luther*, and *The Illustrated Atlas of Native American History*. He is also a major contributor to the *American National Biography*, published by Oxford University Press in 1999. Crompton was a member of the Spirituality in Education conference at Naropa Institute in 1977 and attended the three-hundredth anniversary celebration of Edwards's birth, held in Northampton in 2003.

MARTIN E. MARTY is an ordained minister in the Evangelical Lutheran Church and the Fairfax M. Cone Distinguished Service Professor Emeritus at the University of Chicago Divinity School, where he taught for thirty-five years. Marty has served as president of the American Academy of Religion, the American Society of Church History, and the American Catholic Historical Association, and was also a member of two U.S. presidential commissions. He is currently Senior Regent at St. Olaf College in Northfield, Minnesota. Marty has written more than fifty books, including the three-volume *Modern American Religion* (University of Chicago Press). His book *Righteous Empire* was a recipient of the National Book Award.